Floortime Strategies to Promote Development in Children and Teens

Floortime Strategies to Promote Development in Children and Teens

A User's Guide to the DIR® Model

by

Andrea Davis, Ph.D.

Lahela Isaacson, M.S.

and

Michelle Harwell, M.S.

Baltimore • London • Sydney

Paul H. Brookes Publishing Co.
Post Office Box 10624
Baltimore, Maryland 21285-0624

www.brookespublishing.com

Typeset by Cenveo, Inc., Stamford, Connecticut.
Manufactured in the United States of America by
Sheridan Books, Inc., Chelsea, Michigan.

Cover image ©istockphoto/vitapix

All of the case studies in this book are composites of the authors' actual experiences. In all instances, names and identifying details have been altered to protect confidentiality.

Library of Congress Cataloging-in-Publication Data
The Library of Congress has cataloged the print edition as follows:
Davis, Andrea Lee, 1961–
Floortime strategies to promote development in children and teens: a user's guide to the DIR model / by Andrea Davis, Ph.D.,
Lahela Isaacson, M.S., and Michelle Harwell, M.S.
     pages   cm
  Includes bibliographic references and index.
  ISBN 978-1-59857-734-1 (pbk.)   ISBN 978-1-59857-821-8 (EPUB)
  1. Parents of developmentally disabled children–United States. 2. Developmentally disabled children–mental health–United
States. 3. Developmentally disabled children–psychology–United States. 4. Child psychology–United States. I. Isaacson,
Lahela. II. Harwell, Michelle. III. Title.
  HQ759.913.D39 2014
  306.874–dc23   2014011147

British Library Cataloguing in Publication data are available from the British Library.

2023 2022 2021

10   9   8   7   6   5   4

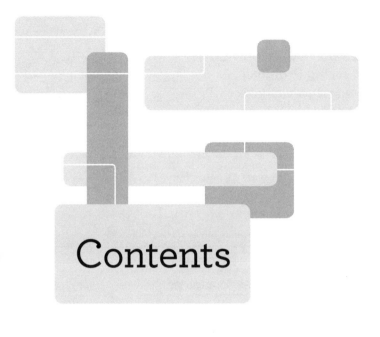

Contents

About the Authors

Andrea Davis, Ph.D., Director and Founder, Greenhouse Therapy Center, 685 East California Boulevard, Pasadena, California 91106

Andrea Davis received her B.A. in psychology from Swarthmore College, M.A. in theology from Fuller Theological Seminary, and Ph.D. in clinical psychology from Fuller Graduate School of Psychology. She completed her postdoctoral fellowship in infant mental health and early childhood disorders at Brown University Medical School. She returned to the west coast to join the UCLA Department of Pediatrics as Director of Research for the FOCUS project intervention study and to open a private practice in Pasadena, California. This practice grew into Greenhouse Therapy Center, a psychological center providing psychotherapy to individual adults, couples, parents, adolescents, and children from an attachment theory perspective. Greenhouse also offers intensive in-home Floortime or relationship-based developmental intervention for children and adolescents with developmental disorders and their families.

Lahela Isaacson, M.S., LMFT, DIRFloortime Supervisor and Program Manager, Greenhouse Therapy Center, 685 East California Boulevard, Pasadena, California 91106

Lahela Isaacson has devoted her professional career to working with children with special needs using the DIRFloortime® model. Ms. Isaacson received her B.A. in psychology from Pepperdine University. She earned her M.S. in marriage and family therapy from Seattle Pacific University. Soon after graduating she was introduced to the DIRFloortime model and was captivated. Ms. Isaacson currently works at Greenhouse Therapy Center as a DIRFloortime supervisor and program manager.

Michelle Harwell, M.S., LMFT, Owner, Michelle Harwell Therapy, 2120 Colorado Boulevard, Suite 2, Los Angeles, California 90041

Michelle Harwell is an expert training leader and supervisor in DIRFloortime and an infant mental health and early intervention specialist. She maintains a thriving private practice in Los Angeles, California, where she sees clients across the age spectrum: infants, children, adolescents, and adults. She also works as an infant mental health consultant at Elizabeth House, where she helped to secure grant funding through the Pasadena Child Health Foundation to provide mother–infant psychotherapy to at-risk homeless mothers. Ms. Harwell received her B.A. in English literature from the University of Oklahoma, M.A. in theology from Fuller Theological Seminary, and M.S. in marriage and family therapy from the Fuller Graduate School of Psychology. She dedicated her postgraduate training to the areas of development, attachment, trauma, and neuroscience and is currently completing her Ph.D in psychoanalysis from The Institute for Contemporary Psychoanalysis. Ms. Harwell is a well-respected speaker, trainer, and supervisor who provides professional development and consultation to therapists and families.

Foreword

Floortime belongs to everyone. Joining in play with a child or adolescent conveys a message: "I am here with you, to find out what interests you, to play with you, and to enter your world. We can tickle or roughhouse and laugh together. We can pretend to be your favorite characters, arm your knights before the pirates get to your castle, or check out your favorite music, videos, or games. I will join you, follow your ideas, and we will play together to feel close, to have fun, to discover, to find the gleam in your eye!"

This book provides strategies and guidance to parents, teachers, therapists, and aides for finding these pathways to each child's heart and mind. The approach presented is called *Floortime* to highlight the importance of real, in-person interactions, although Floortime may take place anywhere—on the floor, on a couch, on a walk. The goal is always to entice a child or a teen into close, warm, interactive relationships. Fostering these relationships is especially important for children with special needs.

Floortime is both a theory and an intervention method. It is the theory at the heart of the DIR® model that Dr. Stanley Greenspan and I created, and it is an intervention method that can be either the primary method or used along with other intervention approaches parents may choose. It is a systematic approach with a sound theoretical model and research-based neuroscientific support for the active ingredients in intervention. The relationships forged during Floortime pave the way for all aspects of development and brings them together. Wooing the child or adolescent into relationships and interaction, understanding his or her individual differences, and tailoring interactions to support engagement are all ways to seize the neuroplasticity of the brain by providing experiences that can create missing neural interconnections. The Floortime strategies in this book illustrate how parents and professionals can build the foundations for the types of relationships that promote lifelong learning.

The DIR model was originally developed through our Clinical Infant Development Program, a longitudinal National Institute of Mental Health study of infants and parents from multi-problem families. Our goal was to offer preventive intervention to newborns in families where prior children had evidenced problems, with the hopes of building better foundations for the newborn and helping families support their children's development. Armed with psychodynamic, cognitive, and social theories of development, we learned about addressing individual differences in sensory motor processing, and we identified the primary active ingredient in supporting development: affect. We then brought this to our work with regulatory and autism spectrum disorders.

The DIR model revolutionized the concept of human development, integrating and synthesizing theories and models from different disciplines into an affect-driven model that captures the essence of every child's needs across his or her lifespan. Every child needs close, loving, supportive, and sensitive relationships to achieve and realize his or her potential. For those individuals with special needs, optimizing relationships requires a unique understanding of how to tailor interventions to their individual profile in order to help them realize their potential. This, of course, can be a significant challenge for many children and adolescents. But the challenge is shared among the parents, clinicians, and scientists who work together to forge connections to allow every child to develop. Attuned relationships carve the pathway through myriad individual differences, environments, cultures, and opportunities. And the essence of the DIR model is to provide the relationships that support development.

The DIR model's focus on foundational developmental capacities is critical for all children—those in high-risk environments, those at risk for autism or other developmental disorders, and those with other special needs. The purpose is to help these children learn from the world around them, to understand how others think and feel, and to start and finish intentional sequences purposefully. These experiences develop common sense, also known as practical intelligence, and complement the emotional thinking encouraged by Floortime.

Page by page, this book will explain the Floortime method to empower parents and their children to advance development. It is suitable for every age across the lifespan since our human needs to learn and relate never cease. The sequential curriculum of strategies in this book offers a simplified way to learn and to teach Floortime and provides several creative ideas for putting Floortime into practice. The art is to integrate these ideas throughout your interactions to support the child's sense of self, agency, and comprehension, all of which can lead to exciting new discoveries. Play blossoms into meaningful conversation as children develop and are ready to talk about their experiences and feelings, their problems and plans, their disappointments, and their dreams and hopes, as they begin to reflect on their reasoning and who they are in relation to others.

Floortime is not automatic by any means—and it takes practice. Observing yourself on video and reflecting on your style with mentors, peers, and supervisors are essential components in making Floortime work, especially since Floortime skills and strategies must evolve as the child gets older and advances developmentally. Perhaps the most essential thing to remember is to share attention and stay engaged and interactive. Even when children or teens can play or converse at higher symbolic levels, if they are not fully engaged, you must drop back down to the level of interaction where they are able to connect and communicate, reestablishing the closeness of the relationship.

At every successive level it is important to keep in mind the DIR concepts and principles highlighted in this book and to consider specific goals for each interaction. In addition, other essential experiences that form the building blocks of development are built into a comprehensive DIR program of intervention designed for a child or adolescent. These experiences include semistructured social problem solving and work activities, sensory motor activities, education and special education, various therapies and models of intervention, playdates, family support, nutrition, and medication when indicated. As children grow, experiences need to be continuously added to develop executive functions and prepare the child for transitioning to adulthood.

This book will surely engage you. Read and reread it often to support your Floortime with children climbing the developmental ladder. You too will surely develop in this lifelong process of personal growth.

Serena Wieder, Ph.D.
Clinical Director, Profectum Foundation
Co-Founder, Interdisciplinary Council of Developmental
and Learning Disorders and the DIR Institute
Co-Author with Stanley Greenspan of *The Child with
Special Needs and Engaging Autism*
Co-Author with *Harry Wachs of Visual Spatial Portals
to Thinking, Feeling and Movement*

How to Use This Book

This book is designed to help professionals and parents more easily grasp and practice basic DIRFloortime® methods at home with children and teens. While the techniques are very useful for advancing the development of all children and adolescents, they are particularly relevant when there are developmental challenges including attention deficit disorder, sensory processing disorder, language delays, motor problems, trauma history, or autism spectrum disorder. We recommend first reading *The Child with Special Needs* by Stanley Greenspan and Serena Wieder (1998) and then getting more in-depth information through ICDL.com and Profectum.org.

The pages here greatly simplify Floortime concepts in order to help you visualize, remember, and put into practice relational strategies that are part of the DIR® approach. The book also simplifies the application of the model by identifying which methods are especially appropriate for each of the nine developmental capacities or milestones. The curriculum of strategies provides individual stand-alone teaching and learning resources in a step-by-step progression. This means any strategy may be selected as needed to address the child's individual differences, the parent's particular skills and needs, or the focus of the current DIRFloortime session.

Each specific strategy has been given a short, memorable, catch-phrase title to help you internalize the overall approach for natural and spontaneous use any time an opportunity arises. We encourage you to further personalize the pages by adding your own notes on your observations and the therapeutic team's recommendations. Use the two introductory chapters to remember and practice the foundational, overarching Floortime strategies that can be used to help all children and teens. Use the subsequent chapters to foster the nine social-emotional milestones or foundational developmental capacities of DIR. Use the varied examples for each strategy to stimulate your own creative ideas for your unique situation. Use the appendix to learn and apply strategies from a variety of parenting approaches to help children and adolescents grow out of problem behaviors.

Introduction

Welcome to a journey of learning a new approach to helping children and teens reach their highest social-emotional and intellectual potential. DIR®, or the Developmental, Individual Differences, Relationship-Based model, is a unique intervention approach developed by Drs. Stanley Greenspan and Serena Wieder as a way for families and professionals to understand and help children, especially those with developmental differences. Floortime is the application of DIR principles to intervene with children and adolescents, by using intentional methods of playing and interacting to help them achieve crucial capacities in personal development. This book is based on DIRFloortime® as presented in *The Child with Special Needs* (S. Greenspan & S. Wieder, 1998; Da Capo Press).

First, professionals and parents evaluate and work with a child's or adolescent's profile of sensory needs and of strengths and weaknesses in language, motor, visual, and intellectual functioning. This understanding helps them adapt activities and interactive styles to optimize the child's or adolescent's abilities.

Next, they evaluate the child's or teen's current social-emotional level in a particular moment and interact with him or her at that level so that they are sure to connect, relate, and be most effective at fostering higher capacities. They join with the young person's natural interests and desires in playful interactions and close relationships, which provide natural motivation to engage in gradually higher developmental stages of normative emotional and intellectual development. Ideally, this can even blossom into a method and avenue to foster the often overlooked spiritual development of the young person.

Most critical is that in DIRFloortime adults learn to evaluate and reflect on their own tendencies in the relationship and thereby become more adaptable and also more able to help the child or teen to become gradually more capable of self-reflection as well. Extensive research in intergenerational transmission of attachment security shows that caregiver self-reflection and self-awareness are essential for providing the attunement and affect regulation that allow children to develop the ability to think about their own minds and the minds of others.

DIRFloortime was developed out of developmental psychology research and applications, making it distinct from prevailing treatment approaches founded upon principles of behaviorism. The goals of DIRFloortime are grand: focus, intimacy, initiative, mutuality, purposefulness, imaginativeness, logical thinking, joy, spontaneity, empathy, and self-awareness. The means to get there are delightful: play combined with warm, attuned relationships. The positive emotions that result are critical for promoting deep learning and widespread brain integration/organization.

Research findings (Casenhiser, Shanker, & Stieben, 2013; Pajareya & Nopmaneej-umruslers, 2011; Solomon, Necheles, Ferch, & Bruckman, 2007) have provided scientific validation for Dr. Greenspan and Dr. Wieder's approach, with many more validation studies underway. Pervasive developmental disorders have been shown to be *disorders of connectivity* characterized by a lack of integration or coordination between complex brain systems. This is because of differences in brain development (e.g., less neuronal pruning for efficiency) and structure (e.g., smaller hemispheric connector or corpus collosum). DIRFloortime strategies were designed to engage all the major brain systems at once and to harness the therapeutic power of affect, or emotion, which plays an integrative role in the brain. From its inception, DIRFloortime has been aimed right at this underlying cause of developmental problems. This explains its unique transformative power.

What Is DIRFloortime?

The DIRFloortime Pyramid (see p. xix) is a graphic representation of Drs. Greenspan and Wieder's model; at our center we use the pyramid with families to make the approach easier to visualize. To sum up the basic idea, we say social-emotional and cognitive growth happens in the following manner:

- Adults in Floortime *attune, engage, respond, expand, pretend, challenge*, and *reflect*.

- Children and teens in Floortime *regulate, connect, reciprocate, communicate, create, think*, and *self-reflect*.

These capacities of adults and children or adolescents—listed here in the order of the chapters of the book—intertwine to support healthy, creative development.

1. When adults *attune* to the child and to themselves, children learn to become *regulated*.

2. When adults *engage* the child, children learn to *connect* emotionally with others.

3. When adults *respond* to the child, children initiate *reciprocal interaction* with others.

4. When adults *expand* the child's initiations, children *communicate* and negotiate with others.

5. When adults enter the *pretend* realm, children learn to imagine and *create* ideas.

6. When adults *challenge* a child to solve emotional and logical problems, children develop *emotional thinking and logical thinking*.

7–9. When adults *reflect* with the child, children learn to *self-reflect* or think broadly and deeply about themselves in relationship to the world.

In this way, adults launch, and children and adolescents grow.

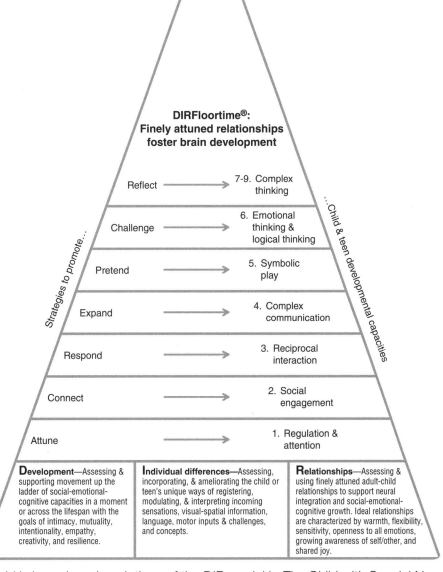

(Pyramid is based on descriptions of the DIR model in *The Child with Special Needs* by Stanley Greenspan and Serena Wieder [Da Capo Press; 1998] and Engaging *Autism* by Stanley Greenspan and Serena Wieder [Da Capo Press; 2006].)

Steps to Begin DIRFloortime Home Intervention

Assessment: Obtain a comprehensive *developmental*[1] evaluation or assessment of your child or teen's individual differences by a medical doctor, clinical psychologist, or multidisciplinary team specializing in developmental differences. The recommendations from the assessment report should help you begin to build an intervention team of the needed professionals and make a plan for school, clinic, and home intervention. This team can work with you to determine important social, emotional, and cognitive developmental goals and strategies.

Focus: Ask the educational and therapeutic team to help you select which pages of this DIRFloortime book might be most appropriate for your situation. You can also use the introductory page of each section to begin your own informal assessment of where you see the needs.

Guidance: Schedule regular sessions with a local (or long-distance) professional who has extensive training and experience in DIR to help you select, apply, and fine-tune the strategies for your family. (Find a professional at ICDLDirectory.com or Profectum.org or PlayProject.org.) This book is not meant as a replacement for working with a professional; it is a helpful supplement for working under the guidance of a professional who has been fully trained through the Interdisciplinary Council on Development and Learning (ICDL) or Profectum.

Update: Have a DIR professional implement the Floortime strategies alongside you or review home video clips to help you monitor ongoing progress, tailor your approach, and select areas for you to work on for your child or teenager and yourself as you each progress.

DIRFloortime Professionals

DIR professionals are trained and certified through the ICDL (ICDL.com) or Profectum (Profectum.org) after they have trained in another related discipline such as medicine, psychology, counseling, education, speech-language pathology, occupational therapy, physical therapy, and so on. They implement the approach described in this book by assessing and intervening with children and adolescents in home, school, or office settings.

More important, they create an affectively attuned, supportive relationship with parents, caregivers, teachers, and educational aides to help them implement Floortime with their children and students. In order to empower parents and

---

[1] Behavioral evaluations are more common; however, they typically focus on problem behaviors. Developmental evaluations are often more appropriate because those with a developmental disorder need professionals who can test and observe them carefully to identify their individual differences or overall profile of challenges, abilities, tendencies, and needs.

caregivers, DIR-trained professionals provide individualized coaching. This coaching ideally is tailored to the caregiver's individual differences, knowledge needs, and best learning style. Coaching may consist of one or more of the following coaching techniques:

- Observing adult–child interaction
- Modeling and demonstration of Floortime strategies for the particular child or adolescent
- Implementing Floortime side by side with the adult
- Offering tips or suggestions in the midst of Floortime interactions
- Recording Floortime and reviewing portions of the video together
- Offering written notes, observations, and suggestions after sessions or video reviews
- Reflecting together on the caregiver's observations of the child or teen and growing self-awareness in the relationship
- Collaborating on devising solutions to problems the child or teen is presenting
- Reviewing progress and setting goals together

To conduct this work well, DIR professionals continually seek out opportunities to reflect on themselves in relationship to their work with others who help them grow in self-awareness.

Overview of the Book's Structure

Core Methods A. Strategies to Promote Social-Emotional and Intellectual Development
Learning to attend to cues, determining and meeting the current stage of social-emotional capacity in any moment and then moving the child or teen up the developmental ladder in each interpersonal interaction

Core Methods B. Understanding and Addressing Individual Differences in Processing Profiles
Observing and using individual differences in sensory, motor, visual, auditory, and language processing capacities

Capacity 1. Regulation and Attention: Attaining a Calm, Alert, Attentive State
Attuning—
Understanding the primary importance of a calm, alert state before expecting anything further in a given moment or in the overall growth trajectory

Capacity 2. Social Engagement: Getting Involved and Connected

Connecting—

Facilitating the component parts of social engagement, including social interest, pleasure, mutual gaze, gestures, attachment, facial affect, initiating and responding to joint attention, clarity of bids, peer and sibling bonding, and more

Capacity 3. Reciprocal Social Interaction: Initiating and Responding Purposefully

Responding—

Supporting the growth of mutuality, reciprocity, and initiative

Capacity 4. Complex Communication: Using Gestures and Words to Solve Problems Together

Expanding—

Instigating extended communication to pave the way for social cooperation and social problem solving

Capacity 5. Symbolic Play: Creating and Using Ideas

Pretending—

Prioritizing the formation of symbols, ideas, and narrative to foster emotional and cognitive growth

Capacity 6. Emotional Thinking and Logical Thinking: Making Sense of Oneself, Others, and the World

Challenging—

Providing opportunities for understanding emotions and for building bridges between ideas to make sense of the world and to develop insight, empathy, judgment, and so on.

Capacities 7–9. Complex Thinking: Multicausal, Gray Area, and Reflective Thinking

Reflecting—

Helping children and adolescents to think with more precision, nuance, and subtlety about the self, others, and the world

Appendix. Reducing Problem Behaviors

Supporting—

Providing for individualized needs and offering supports that help children and teens grow out of problem behaviors

Acknowledgments

This book is based on the lifelong pioneering work of Drs. Stanley Greenspan and Serena Wieder, who developed DIRFloortime® as a beautiful way to help children and parents grow. The articulation of the approach in the form of strategies has been developed and tested through active use with families, Floortime specialists, field supervisors, and clinical supervisors at Greenhouse Therapy Center in Pasadena, California. We thank Serena Wieder, Clinical Director at Profectum, for providing an introduction to this manual. Thanks to Dr. Cecilia Breinbauer, former Director of the Interdisciplinary Council on Development and Learning (ICDL), and to Jeff Guenzel, its current CEO, for giving approval for this project. We thank the Profectum team, including Clinical Director Serena Wieder and Executive Director Monica Osgood, for their enthusiastic support. We have learned the most from the faculty and students in the DIR institutes and online courses sponsored by ICDL, especially Rachel Morse, Monica Osgood, Joshua Feder, Barbara Kalmanson, Michele Ricamato, Diane Cullinane, Rosemary White, and Mona Delahooke. We have also learned so many helpful parenting strategies from Noel Janis-Norton of the Calmer, Easier, Happier Parenting Centre in London. For their direct input on the early or late stages of developing the book, we thank Susan Reed, Cynthia Davis, Cherisse Sherin, Jodi Peterson, and Ashley Wilkins.

Michelle Harwell thanks her teachers and mentors Andrea Davis, Cynthia Davis, and Connie Lillas for introducing her to the wonder and possibilities of play.

Lahela Isaacson thanks her mentors Cynthia Davis and Andrea Davis as well as the parents and families of children with special needs that she has known both professionally and personally. She is also grateful to God, her hope and joy.

Andrea Davis thanks all of her former and current therapeutic and administrative staff at Greenhouse Therapy Center for giving all of their hearts to this wonderful work. She also thanks her mentors in practice and research: Linda Wagener, Winston Gooden, Barry Lester, Charles Zeanah, and Marianne Barton. In the end she is most grateful to God, who imagined, established, and continues to sustain Greenhouse Therapy Center as a place of healing, hope, and growth for so many.

Basic Strategies to Promote Social-Emotional and Intellectual Development

Core Methods A is designed as an overview of the main principles or core strategies of the DIRFloortime® approach to promoting social-emotional and intellectual development. These core methods will help you visualize and implement the basics of the DIRFloortime approach at any point along the continuum of development. Some of these methods will be addressed in more detail later in the curriculum, when they are presented as a way to promote a particular social-emotional milestone or developmental capacity.

To get a general idea of how to use Floortime to promote social-emotional and intellectual development, it is important to understand all of the basic methods presented in Core Methods A. No matter where your child or teen is on the developmental ladder, it will help to understand and practice each of the methods.

Basic Strategies

The general Floortime methods to promote social-emotional and intellectual development are as follows:

A.1. **Follow cues:** Provide sensitive interactions by following cues.
A.2. **Be responsive:** Always respond to all communication.
A.3. **Build upward:** Meet your child or teen at current developmental capacity.
A.4. **Use play:** Use play and playfulness as a primary means to engage and teach.
A.5. **Use natural interests:** Capitalize on natural interests to elicit higher skills.
A.6. **Use problems:** Set up situations that invite child-initiated solutions.
A.7. **Pretend play:** Create opportunities to use ideas in symbolic (pretend) play.
A.8. **Embrace feelings:** Help embrace a wide range of feelings.
A.9. **Enrich ideas:** Help enrich ideas or stories in play and conversation.
A.10. **Self-reflect:** Take a reflective stance toward yourself in interactions.

Follow Cues

 A.1 Provide sensitive interactions by following cues

Why?

Following the child's or teen's verbal and nonverbal cues allows us to tune into individual differences and to tailor our interactions to current needs. Sensitive care-givers provide many experiences of attunement, misattunement, and rapid repair or reattunement. This may be described as *relational choreography*. Research findings in developmental psychology and attachment theory show that, in cultures all across the world, a sensitive caregiver gives the child a much higher likelihood of a lifelong sense of security and the capacity for warm, close relationships. Children who feel this emotional security at home are observed to be significantly more successful with peers and in academic pursuits later on.

How do we get there?

- Take your time: Slow your own tempo, put aside your many distractions and thoughts, ground yourself, and wake up to being fully present with your child or adolescent.

- Listen and watch: Observe carefully to understand your child's way of seeing the world. Facial expressions, tone of voice, gestures, body posture, and words (or lack of them) are all important clues that help you determine how to approach a child or adolescent in a particular moment. For example, is his or her behavior relaxed and outgoing? Withdrawn or uncommunicative? Bubbling with excitement?

- Adjust: Once mood and style have been assessed, you can approach interaction with the appropriate tone, volume, tempo, words, or gestures.

- Repair: When the relational connection gets disrupted, find ways to initiate a repair so the child or teen learns to feel that attachments are robust and resilient.

©istockphoto/NiDerLander

Examples

Infant: As you lean in and begin vocalizing to your baby, she turns her head away slightly to the left. You notice that when you pull your face back and continue making the sounds you know she likes, your baby turns her head back toward you to make eye contact and giggles.

Preschooler: You watch carefully while playing together and notice the child is less responsive to your smiles when he is seated on the ground and your gaze is aimed downward at him, so you help him play the same game standing up while looking across the table at one another.

School-age student: Your daughter gets aggressive with her younger brother before you head out the door almost every Monday morning. You have a simple talk with her Sunday night to show your emotional understanding of how hard Mondays can feel when you have to head back to school or work. Then you and she make a plan for 30 minutes of special time to look forward to after school on Mondays.

Teen: You notice your son gets really quiet and unresponsive on the way to an extracurricular activity. You slow yourself and let go of the pressure of the sched-ule in order to check in with him—what might he be apprehensive about, and how could he handle the situation with extra help if needed?

Be Responsive

A.2 Always respond to all communication

Why?

Responsiveness, or responding to *everything* children and adolescents communicate nonverbally or verbally, is a hallmark of a growth-promoting relationship. Developmental psychologists have proven that relationships are the context for growth and learning. Responsive relationships do this best—even children with severe developmental delays have better overall outcomes if they are securely attached to their parent in the early years. And securely attached children are those whose parents are sensitive and responsive to the child's emotional states. Moreover, sensitively following the child's lead, or being responsive, creates a sense of social influence or efficacy. Responding to each communication builds a core human capacity to share minds and feel warmly connected to others now and in the future.

How do we get there?

- Value: Treat each word or gesture as important.

- Be a responder: A young person will learn to initiate more often if you respond.

- Don't change the topic: A longer flow of communication will develop if you follow up on the child's action or idea without switching gears.

- Respond in kind: Your response must be dependent on what the child communicated to you; this will teach your child or teen how to feel "on the same page" with others.

Examples

Preverbal: A child is crawling under the table and then grunts. You ask, "Oh, stuck?" He looks up, half smiles, and grunts louder. You affirm, "Oh, no, you are really stuck." He whines. You ask, "Okay, you want help?" He says, "Help!" You respond, "Okay, I'll help." One small vocalization becomes conversation, and more conversations will follow.

Nonverbal: A student hands over her attempt at drawing the playground. The one-to-one aide says, "Oh, you finished. I see you worked hard on your drawing." The student frowns. The aide asks, "You don't agree?" The student sharply shakes her head side to side. The aide says, "You look like you don't like how it came out." The student hands her crayon to the aide. The aide asks, "You want me to help?" The student stares at the drawing. The aide says, "I could add something to the playground, but where would you like it to go?" The student gets distracted and starts watching other students. The aide says, "Yes, I see everyone else, too, but we can sit and finish this if you like. Hmmm, I'm wondering where to draw on this." The student looks back and pats the middle of the paper. The aide says, "Okay, right here? I'll put something right in the middle. What should I put there?" The aide offers a communication device to the student, who types part of her name. "Oh, okay," says the aide. "I can add *you* there on the playground." Every communication was valued, every response maintained the flow by responding to the child's communication, and every response helped to draw out a shared idea and then create a conversation.

Verbal: The child says, "Yuck!" The adult (wisely prioritizing basic communication skills to be addressed long before lessons on manners) asks, "You hate this pasta sauce?" The child says, "Yeah, yucky." The adult tables hurt feelings in favor of a higher conversational goal and asks, "You like plain?" The child says, "Yay!" The adult (working on communication before a later goal of flexibility) asks, "Would you like plain pasta tonight?" The child says, "Yes, please." The adult says, "Okay, while you eat some veggies, I'll get some plain noodles for you."

Build Upward

A.3 Meet your child or teen at current developmental capacity

Why?

Development happens in a series of stages, and each stage builds on the prior ones. Similarly, in each particular moment, a child or adult must be functioning well on the lower rungs of the developmental ladder to do very well at the upper rungs; for example, one cannot expect a person to be able to show good social problem solving and emotional reasoning if basic regulation and engagement are challenged in the moment. This is especially true in new situations calling for a new social-emotional or intellectual ability. New abilities must be built from a strong base foundation, so to foster solid and consistent growth in each moment, build upward from the ground floor.

How do we get there?

Stop and think: Are you and the child or adolescent doing first things first?

- Is she regulated?

- Is he sharing joint attention?

- Is she engaged with me?

- Is our communication flowing back and forth?

- Is he solving problems together with me or others?

- Is she making logical and emotional connections?

©istockphoto/Imageegaml

Examples

General developmental capacity:

Play Peekaboo, even with a 4-year-old, if that's what works to increase his or her capacity for sharing pleasure and attention.

Momentary developmental capacity:

Teach a concept only after a child or adolescent is calm and engaged.

Invite pretend play only after a child is open to sharing ideas and pleasurable emotions together with you.

Invite discussion about what went wrong in a tantrum after the child or teen is re-regulated, engaging in back-and-forth communication, able to access symbolic capacities (words), and able to make emotional connections and logical connections. For example:

You ask, "You were mad because we couldn't finish the game?"
The child says, "Yes!"
You say, "Show us how mad you were, but remember the no-hurting rule."
The child punches the couch cushion, then smiles, feeling understood.

Use Play

 A.4 Use play and playfulness as primary means to engage and teach

Why?

To facilitate development, we must become fluent in play. Children, teens, and even adults are more mentally flexible and open to learning when they enter shared states of joy. Motivating any person to change—getting people to start doing what is difficult for them—is one of the hardest problems in the world to solve. Play is bonding and naturally motivating, as it brings with it feel-good hormones released by laughter, surprise, movement, challenge, success, and positive and warm social encounters. Engaging a child and teaching through play ensures willingness, cooperation, and effort. It also ensures better learning because the positive emotions support more successful memory encoding across different brain regions and systems.

How do we get there?

- Woo younger and older children into interaction rather than demand their attention.

- Watch for the "gleam in the eye" as a sign of interest and delight—then you'll know you can call for a slightly higher capacity and thereby move together up the developmental ladder.

- Remember that you can make mundane moments fun. Approach problems or daily tasks with a gleam in your own eye.

- When both of you are having fun, you can be sure that learning can begin to happen.

Use Play

©istockphoto/oksun70

Examples

Woo: Instead of directing and demanding, "Yoohoo, Joe! Joe? Over here! Look at me!" and say, "Goodness! Here comes Mr. Pointerfinger. He's going to poke you! Ooooh, here he comes! Ouch! He poked *my* eye!"

Be goofy: Instead of "Here's your milk," try "Oh, okay you want more milk. But where did that milk carton go? Is it in your bellybutton? Is it in your armpit? Is it in…?"

Join: Your teen has earned an hour of screen time for finishing a developmentally appropriate amount of homework. You can sit and watch him beat a level in his game or play against him for a few minutes before returning to your own tasks. Your little one loves baseball teams. Play indoor baseball for two runs before school. Your middle one loves trains. Sit down and help build the track and talk about it together.

Create: Your preteen hates cleaning her room and is prone to tantrums. Before any distress, you suggest, "Let's both put on aprons and housekeeping hats, pretend we are cleaning your hotel room as fast as we can, then ask Mom to inspect it and give us a tip if we pass."

Practice: If your child is learning to share and get along with a peer, create a play scenario where Batman and Spider-Man have to take turns or resolve an argument.

Enlighten: Your school-age child is figuring out the confusing dynamics that Greenspan and Salmon (1994) called "playground politics." You can role play out what to do when "Nobody wants to play with me!", "I just want them to do it my way," or "They didn't play with me, so they aren't my friends anymore!"

Use Natural Interests

 Capitalize on natural interests to elicit higher skills

Why?

Utilizing natural interests and passions is a key motivational strategy for moving kids up the developmental ladder. This principle distinguishes DIRFloortime from other approaches. Since affect or emotion is a natural physiological integrator of neurological processes, using the interests and passions that activate positive feelings will help to accomplish the all-important brain integration. Capitalizing on a child's or teen's natural motivation will allow for more rich interaction and sustained engagement.

How do we get there?

- Follow your child's or adolescent's emotional lead by asking yourself what he or she already loves to do.

- Watch what he or she does in spare moments and free time.

- Use those activities to engage the child or teen with you and draw out higher capacities.

©Veer/Ocean Photography

Examples

Preschooler: If you find your baby or child gets attentive and alert when you play music at home or in the car, then make up songs about your daily routines to teach new vocabulary or make up songs about the day to provide advance warning and help with routines.

School-age child: If he loves climbing on the couch, engage him in planning how to make the area safe for climbing and build a climbing obstacle course together.

Preteen: If she loves being in motion, push her on a swing while you talk about her day.

Teen: If he is fascinated by airports, get permission from teachers to tailor most writing assignments to involve that interest area.

Use Problems

 ## Set up situations that invite child-initiated solutions

Why?

Setting up problem-solving situations in the everyday environment creates opportunities for children and adolescents to learn initiation and to practice the sort of thinking that must be developed in order to solve problems. They will often be most motivated and determined to solve imaginary problems that can be inserted into play scenarios or to solve mini-problems which adults can allow to arise in daily living. This sort of practice in play and daily life can pave the way for solving more abstract academic problems. Also, active engagement in thinking and solving makes the learning more integrated with other knowledge and therefore more permanent.

How do we get there?

- Be curious: "We finished that game—now what?" "His face looks upset! How could we make it better?" (The key words here are *what* and *how*.)

- Presume competence: Assume the child or adolescent has emotional and intellectual competencies that can only be demonstrated given the right opportunity and supports.

- Don't be Mr./Mrs. Fix-it: Elicit ideas about how to solve the problem, underline and expand the feeling they're having in the moment, and support them in the steps of problem solving. Don't solve the problem for them.

- Feign confusion: Pretending to be quite ignorant and slow to understand provides opportunities for them to practice problem solving and to interact with you.

Examples

Be curious: If she spills her juice, say, "Uh oh, what should we do? How could we get this cleaned up? Okay, so I get a rag, and then what?"

Don't be Mr./Mrs. Fix-it: Your older child's science assignment is to design a miniature race car. You see that the car is too heavy to move. Instead of starting to solve the problem yourself by explaining that it's too heavy or beginning to make it lighter yourself, say, "Oh, your car won't move? Why do you think it's getting stuck?" If the child offers no ideas, suggest, "Is it maybe something about the wheels? Or the size?"

Feign confusion: When you're about to drive your child somewhere, buckle up in the backseat next to him and put on a "waiting face." When he wonders what you're doing, say, "How are we going to get to the park?" or "Hey, who's driving this car?"

Use skill games: Use semistructured play and interaction to address any age child's weaker areas. For example, if motor planning is a difficulty, set up obstacle course races; if visual-spatial processing is a weakness, play hide-and-search games regularly.

Pretend Play

A.7 Create opportunities to use ideas in symbolic (pretend) play

Why?

Pretend play isn't just for fun. It facilitates creativity, initiative, abstract thinking, problem solving, and emotional comprehension. The first steps into pretend are a child's first deliberate attempts at creating new ideas. Higher levels of pretending allow for integrating ideas with feelings and thereby coming to a more sophisticated understanding of oneself and the world. The highest levels of pretending are required for human beings to create new solutions to difficult problems in math, science, interpersonal situations, and society.

How do we get there?

- Capture and capitalize on natural interests.

- Incorporate sensory needs into the pretend play to make it more enticing and easier to sustain.

- Involve yourself as an active player.

- Highlight the emotional content of the play.

©istockphoto/KellyBoreson

Examples

Young child: Add a voice and a viewpoint to help the child engage with a toy or object symbolically: "I'm Sammy the Spoon! PLEEEASE don't eat me….oh, NO!!"

School-age child: Inject pretend into mundane tasks: "The toothpaste is a white worm; can you trap it with your toothbrush?" Give inanimate objects a life: "Your bear is over there all alone; do you think he is sad? Does he want to go with us to the dentist?" Join in the pretend as a character: "Okay, if you're Thomas, how about I be Percy?"

Teen: Use stories and videos to help adolescents create new ideas: "What would have been a better ending to the Spider-Man movie? What would be a great prequel story for it?"

Embrace Feelings

A.8 Help embrace a wide range of feelings

Why?

Teaching children and adolescents to embrace all kinds of feelings facilitates emotional self-awareness, emotional intelligence, emotional regulation, and emotional comprehension of others. British psychoanalyst and child development researcher John Bowlby (1940) first taught how secure attachment can be fostered by parents who are accepting of all of the child's feelings and experience. They teach their children to be similarly open and available to what exists inside themselves and others. Embracing all of our feelings is a key to a healthy emotional life and meeting the social, academic, work, and spiritual challenges in life.

How do we get there?

- Believe and teach that emotions are not good or bad; they just are. It's what we do with them that matters.

- Notice the feelings your child or adolescent does not acknowledge. Include the excluded feelings in positive, pleasurable moments in your play sessions, your time spent reading books together, and your conversations.

- Express and comment on your own varied feelings.

- Look out for opportunities to encounter and discuss a gradually widening variety of feelings in play, books, and conversation.

Examples

Preverbal child: Ask, "Mad? Mad at brother?"

Nonverbal child: Write two feelings options on an erasable board and have the child point to show how he or she is feeling. Ask, "Are you feeling worried? Sad?"

Verbal child: Say, "You look pretty excited about this party!!"

Verbal child who has lost access to words: Say, "You're not eating very much tonight. I wonder if you might be sad about missing your friend after the move. It's okay to be sad—I'm sad his family is moving away, too, because I'm going to miss them."

Enrich Ideas

A.9 Help enrich ideas or stories in play and conversation

Why?

Elaborating ideas facilitates creativity, conversational ability, and logical thinking. It takes kids from producing simple ideas to being able to reason and ponder from a place of depth and complexity.

How do we get there?

- Support and extend but don't be in the lead.

- Lend your enthusiasm to extend the thinking.

- Set up problems to be solved.

- Add complexity, twists, and drama in play.

- Throw a monkey wrench into conversations.

Enrich Ideas

©istockphoto/noblige

Examples

Help to make play more interesting: "You said it was a Christmas train. Hmmm, I wonder if it needs us to make some packages to transport? Want to ask the conductor if he would stop to pick up some big, shiny packages?"

Expand the story: The child or teen begins to tell a familiar story, so you can use large gestures to slow him or her down and begin to wonder together more deeply about each character's motivation and intent. For example, you might scratch your head, shrug, and say something like, "Your robot always wins the battle because…?"

Challenge a simple explanation of a conflict at school: "He is a mean guy? Is he always mean? He was nice when he came over here to hang out—what do you think made him act mean at the skate park?"

Self-Reflect

A.10 Take a reflective stance toward yourself in interactions

Why?

Self-reflection is the hallmark of DIR®. Self-reflection is essential for effectively supporting the development of a child or young person because it helps the adult become more open and emotionally present to the entire spectrum of the child's internal experiences, emotions, and needs. Parental self-awareness is also one of the keys to developing children's self-awareness and resulting self-control. Unresolved pain in the parent's past always interferes with accurate reading of and sensitive responding to offspring's emotional cues, and research shows that those offspring end up carrying surprisingly parallel emotional limitations (Main, Kaplan, & Cassidy, 1985; Wallin, 2007). Thus, the work that parents do to resolve their past pain in an effort to build an integrated, open, coherent narrative of their own identity and personal history is a major predictor of their offspring's future capacity to stay open, close, and connected in key relationships. Use Figure A.1 as a guide for regular journaling about your experiences and growth in Floortime with your child or adolescent.

How do we get there?

- Pay attention to your own states of regulation and dysregulation.

- Take a curious, nonjudgmental, compassionate stance toward your own emotional challenges.

- Consider your emotional and relational history, including family legacies, reactivities, habits, and blind spots.

- Journal about your Floortime moments, reflecting on yourself and your past as it interacts with the present.

- Talk to understanding members of your support system or a caring professional. Share your self-observations in order to gradually develop a coherent narrative or accurate and full explanation of yourself and your own personal history and parenting style.

©istockphoto/psdphotography

Examples

A sample journal entry:

July 7: Morning DIRFloortime after other kids dropped at school—bath idea was excellent—the warm water and the sounds seemed to keep Aaron more alert and able to focus on shared ideas. A few moments of shared pleasure about whale and fishing boat play with lovely eye contact and what seemed like some intentional vocal attempts to communicate—but I noticed myself shutting down a little emotionally, or not engaging/expanding, when his squeals got really loud. Is this my own auditory oversensitivity to sound? (Bathroom is really echo-y.) Or is it more about my own sadness about the utter lack of shared joy in my early years? (The feeling that it was prohibited and maybe should be prohibited if it gets "too good?") So maybe I can talk more to Dave or to Dr. Natalie about this to sort it out by talking it out?

Date:_____   Time:_____

Length of Session:_____

What were my goals for my child in this Floortime session?
1.
2.
3.
What strategies seemed to work best to support those goals?
1.
2.
3.
What did I learn about my child?

What were my goals for myself in this session?
1.
2.
What did I learn about myself?

Questions for therapeutic team:

Figure A.1. Floortime journal.

Understanding and Addressing Individual Differences in Processing Profiles

Children and teens have unique, neurologically determined ways of taking in, managing, and interacting with the stimuli coming from the world around them. They have unique ways of *processing sensations*, meaning adapting to and making sense of sight; sound; touch; taste; gravity; information from skin, joints, and limbs; body positioning; motion; temperature; and emotions. They also have unique capacities or challenges in the ability to plan and carry out actions and ideas, or *motor planning and sequencing*. Similar differences in visual-spatial integration, language input and output, balance, coordination, memory, comprehension, and executive functioning affect how the child interacts with the environment.

DIRFloortime® is distinct from other therapeutic approaches in that it helps you think about your child's unique profile or pattern of neurobiological strengths and weaknesses and provides you with insight into how you can tailor the environment and relational interactions to promote optimal development. Floortime sessions are designed to help you make use of your child's or teen's *sensory processing profile* as well as to practice expanding language, motor, visual, sensory processing, and cognitive capacities.

This introductory section describes some of the basic approaches of Floortime to understanding and addressing individual differences. It is important to practice the strategies listed here in Core Methods B in order to comprehend and use the whole Floortime approach.

Individual Differences

The general principles behind Floortime's approach to understanding and addressing individual differences in processing profiles are as follows:

B.1. **Child's profile:** Identify and understand your child's or teen's profile of strengths and weaknesses.

B.2. **Adult's profile:** Consider your individual differences.

B.3. **Adapt yourself:** Adapt your interactive style to your child's or teen's unique profile.

B.4. **Calm or energize:** Provide motor or sensory inputs as needed to calm or energize.

B.5. **Home design:** Set up the home environment to accommodate the unique sensory profile.

B.6. **Sensory connections:** Provide daily sensory-motor relational experiences.

B.7. **Practice in play:** Provide daily planned play activities to address processing challenges.

Child's Profile

B.1 Identify and understand your child's or teen's profile of strengths and weaknesses

Why?

To help children and teens progress, we must understand, incorporate, and allow for how they process the various stimuli coming from the world. Once professionals have pinpointed their specific strengths and challenges, we can learn how to use those strengths or preferences to work through or around the challenges. See Figure B.1 for a sample assessment of a child's individual differences and how they support or restrict each developmental capacity.

How do we get there?

- Remember OWL: Observe, watch, and listen.

- Keep a journal of your observations.

- Keep notes on professionals' feedback on the child's or teen's profile.

- Share your journal or notes with your team to get ideas.

- Pass on the profile to others on the team such as teachers and relatives to empower them to understand and work well with your child or adolescent.

©GeDy Images/Blend Images

Examples

Reports from the psychologist, occupational therapist, speech therapist, developmental optometrist, developmental pediatrician, or school assessment team all provide data that can be simplified into a short list to share with team members and family. After just a few Floortime sessions, one parent in Indonesia caught the vision and went home and made a cheery wall poster complete with illustrative photos to explain her extremely sensitive daughter's individual profile to grandparents, aunts, and uncles so they would understand better how to interact with her and not to judge her.

Sample profile:

Spinning in a circle, chewing on chips or pretzels, or sucking on ice chips all up-regulate Sarah for alertness and attention before reading/math.

Lower pitched voices are easier for her to follow; high-pitched sounds are too intense and need to be limited.

Visual distraction or clutter is overstimulating; simplify the visual field to increase her mental organization and attention to task.

Proprioceptive inputs (pulling on a stretch band or putting firm pressure on her shoulders or hips) all ground her and reduce her anxiety in peer groups.

Breaks for deep breathing help Sarah access her words and logic in sibling or peer conflict.

Capacity	Child ("Joshua," age 12)	Adult's ability to facilitate the capacity (Parent—"Miriam")
1. Regulation and attention *Present*	**Which individual differences may cause constrictions?** Joshua shows hypersensitivity to auditory and visual stimulation (loud/bright computer games increase dysregulation). Craves vestibular input when stressed. **Strengths that support this capacity:** J is aware of his sensory needs and usually seeks helpful sensory input to regulate, using co-regulation with Mom or Grandpa when stressed. Able to remain regulated across a variety of situations and affects. Gross motor planning strengths.	**Which individual differences may cause constrictions?** J's mother Miriam struggles with identifying J's regulation state when he is expressing negative affect, occasionally interpreting mild irritation or sadness as dysregulation before J becomes dysregulated. Working on Strategy 1.5. **Strengths that support the child in this capacity:** Generally attuned to J's regulation state. Able to adjust tone, pitch, volume, and pacing of speech, gesturing, and affect to support regulation. Self-aware of her own regulation states. Uses Strategies 1.1, 1.2, and 1.6.
2. Social engagement *Present*	**Which individual differences may cause constrictions?** When unknown individuals move or speak quickly, J occasionally is unable to maintain shared attention, withdrawing to solitary activities until the person becomes less animated/fast. **Strengths that support this capacity:** Motivated to woo and be wooed across a variety of situations and topics. Interested in the actions and interests of other people.	**Which individual differences may cause constrictions?** Intense work schedule. Sometimes too tired to make efforts at establishing shared attention. **Strengths that support the child in this capacity:** Lively and engaging play and conversation partner. Has learned how to modify affect and gesture to age-appropriate and developmentally appropriate levels as J has progressed. Supports J's ability to assert his preferences. Uses Strategies 2.1, 2.3, 2.6, and 2.7.
3. Reciprocal social interaction *Present*	**Which individual differences may cause constrictions?** Expressive language difficulties and slower to find words and initiate interaction, which interfere with expectable rhythm in conversation. **Strengths that support this capacity:** Comprehension of spoken language and gestures is strong. Slow language production is compensated for with extra gesturing and facial expressiveness, which engages conversation and play partners.	**Which individual differences may cause constrictions?** When she is tired, M occasionally prefers responding to positive communications rather than the full range of J's affect. **Strengths that support the child in this capacity:** Wonderful pacing. Utilizes and responds to facial expression, gestures, and language in her play and conversations. Uses Strategies 3.1, 3.2, and 3.3.
4. Complex communication *Present*	**Which individual differences may cause constrictions?** Slow expression limits J's negotiating and reaching compromise in social conflict situations, particularly when peers and nonattuned adults speak quickly or become impatient with J's slower expression. **Strengths that support this capacity:** Maintains regulation in the face of negative affect in peers and others. Able to ask for more time if the situation is moving too fast: "Let me think for a minute."	**Which individual differences may cause constrictions?** Occasionally solves problems for J, not engaging the "just right challenge" due to time or patience limits. Working on Strategies 4.5 and 4.6. **Strengths that support the child in this capacity:** Highly values self-expression and vigorous interaction. Advocates clearly and strongly for J to have a voice in family and school environments. Teaches others to adjust their pace and patience to adapt to his slower speed. Uses Strategies 4.1 and 4.7.

Figure B.1. Assessing developmental capacities and individual differences.

Capacity	Child ("Joshua," age 12)	Adult's ability to facilitate the capacity (Parent—"Miriam")
5. Symbolic play *Mostly present*	**Which individual differences may cause constrictions?** When attempting to explain a symbolic play idea verbally, the difficulties forming the words and phrases can override the formed idea, causing J to forget. This can cause frustration and some dysregulation. **Strengths that support this capacity:** When provided sufficient time to express ideas in conversation or play, this is an area of strength. Has a rich symbolic world. Able to maintain detailed and elaborate pretend play themes for extended periods of time. More recently has begun to show great creativity at writing short stories with complex plots.	**Which individual differences may cause constrictions?** Still feels hindered by childhood family taboos regarding role-playing dramatic play. Working on Strategies 5.1, 5.2, and 5.6. **Strengths that support the child in this capacity:** M understands importance of imagination and symbolic play for overall maturation. Reads and enjoys nonfiction books with J. Uses Strategy 5.4.
6. Emotional thinking and logical thinking *Mostly present*	**Which individual differences may cause constrictions?** Expressive language difficulties create a gap in connecting ideas. Ideas in conversation and writing are only partially bridged. **Strengths that support this capacity:** Emotional thinking is a strength, with J expressing (predominantly through affect and gesture) a full range of positive and negative emotions. When connecting ideas, J also shows logical idea progression.	**Which individual differences may cause constrictions?** Uncomfortable with negative affect themes such as aggression, assertion, power, conflict, and loss. Working on Strategies 6.1–6.4. **Strengths that support the child in this capacity:** M is highly fluent and logical in thought and demonstrates clear, orderly articulation of reasoning that others can participate in and critique without disruption. Uses Strategies 6.6 and 6.7.
7–9. Complex thinking— multicausal, gray area, and reflective thinking *Emerging*	**Which individual differences may cause constrictions?** When the situation is particularly complex, J struggles with expressing more than three to four of the multiple causes, likely due to difficulty forming the thought, but has expressed a desire to try without help. Difficulties with gray area thinking. Tends to use polarized thinking. **Strengths that support this capacity:** J seems able to utilize emotional thinking and a rich symbolic world to think about the different causes for concrete events creatively. Able to self-reflect in more concrete terms, mostly sensory and regulation differences across time: "I used to react like this; I know I might react like this again in this situation."	**Which individual differences may cause constrictions?** M unlikely to devote time to reflective thinking or encouraging self-reflection. Working on 7, 8, and 9. **Strengths that support the child in this capacity:** Intellectual strength and academic training in law that required many years of practice at refined and nuanced ways of understanding social realities.

Adult's Profile

B.2 Consider your individual differences

Why?

Just as your child or adolescent has unique, biologically based ways of taking in the world, so do you. You may have some irregularities in your ways of managing and processing stimuli and information. Increasing awareness of your own patterns will help you to remain regulated and engaged. See Figure B.1 for a sample assessment of how an adult's profile of individual differences can support or restrict the facilitation of the child's capacities.

How do we get there?

- Think about the similarities and differences between yourself and your child or teen in each of the individual differences categories.

- For example, how fast do you process incoming information compared to your child? How quickly do you express your thoughts? Are you outpacing your child?

- Consider carefully how your own differences enhance or limit your ability to help your child or teen with each social-emotional capacity.

Examples

Auditory differences: If you are oversensitive to sound, you will be less attuned to your child or teenager and to yourself in certain sound-intense environments (rooms with hard surfaces or high ceilings or loud traffic noise). Use sound dampening environments, such as a wall-to-wall carpeted room, for most of your Floortime sessions.

Motor differences: One dad in the United States, upon reviewing video of Floortime sessions together with his DIR® professional, was able to reflect on his own motor planning challenges (e.g., balance, coordination) and how those created significant anxiety during Floortime play with his daughter. He related this to memories from childhood in family and school settings. This awareness gave him compassion for himself and freed him up to try to join his daughter's sensory-motor play with more understanding for his own anxieties and insecurities.

Regulatory differences: Another parent in Canada was able to be honest with herself that symbolic play with small toys was overly down-regulating for her "sleepy" neurology to the point of lulling her to sleep. First, she made sure to always drink either a soda or a coffee with sufficient caffeine about 30 minutes before Floortime as a favor to herself and her child. Next, her Floortime developmental interventionist helped her to see that she was more capable of expanding her child's ideas if she spent some of the Floortime sessions in gross motor play outdoors to activate her creative self.

Adapt Yourself

B.3 Adapt your interactive style to your child's or teen's unique profile

Why?

When an adult adapts his or her interactive style, it enables children or teens to be at their best. They will be most accessible and responsive when you adapt your style to their processing style. This approach also helps the adult (e.g., teacher, parent, therapist) to be more patient, understanding, and less critical and thus to facilitate more transformative learning moments through supportive interaction.

How do we get there?

- Create a unique approach to interacting with your child or teen by taking his or her unique profile into account. Tailor the way you interact with your adolescent or child to his or her specific needs by adjusting your intensity, volume, tempo and pacing, positioning, scheduling, verbal complexity, and so forth.

©istockphoto/Stuartb

Examples

Sight: Try adjusting the speed of your movement so that the child or teen is able to process (follow and make sense of) your actions. Perhaps change the lighting or try playing in a bare room.

Sound: Adapt the tone, speed, and volume of your speech; try playing in a quieter or louder environment.

Touch: Experiment with objects that have various feels (e.g., squishy, hard, gooey) like playdough, rocks, or cotton balls.

Smell: Be aware of the perfume, cologne, soap, candles, and other odor sources in your environment and increase or decrease based on your child's profile.

Taste: Honor preferences for intense tastes or for bland foods; offer new tastes in tiny quantities at the start of a meal.

Body awareness: Give deep squeezes, pillow squishes, light stroking, or tight hugs. Run, jump, and swing depending on the child's motor abilities and needs.

Gravity: Experiment with different types of motion such as vertical jumping, circular swinging, parallel swinging, rapid jiggling motion, and so forth.

Language: Simplify your speech to be just slightly more advanced than the child's or teen's expressive ability.

Calm or Energize

B.4 Provide motor or sensory inputs as needed to calm or energize

Why?

You can help your child or adolescent be in the just-right zone, meaning both alert enough and calm enough to learn and grow in a situation. Using the body and the senses is the easiest way to calm or energize a person.

How do we get there?

- Think first: Is she calm? Is he alert?

- Use observations of your child's or teen's unique profile in your interactions with him or her when you want to wake up the senses (up-regulate) or when they need to be calmed (down-regulate).

Examples:

Underreactive: Have the child or teen engage with you in "heavy work," such as wheelbarrow walking on hands while you hold his or her feet up, floor pushups or wall pushups, pushing games against one another, moving furniture, pushing other people across the floor in laundry baskets, and so forth. This wakes his or her body up, which allows for better relational connection.

Overreactive: You can experiment with sensations that organize and soothe a child or teen's sensory system. For example, compress the shoulder and hip joints toward the center of the body with your hands to calm him or her; practice yoga poses and breathing; give deep pressure in specific areas (e.g., hands, feet), broad areas (whole back), or whole body (which you could squash under couch cushions).

Combination: If the child or adolescent is both underattentive and overactive, you may find some success with vestibular and proprioceptive activity combined. Examples are jumping on a trampoline, being swung in a blanket, or even having the child or teen pumping him- or herself to swing very high on a playground swing. These combination activities can help achieve the just-right regulation balance required before attempting an academic task that demands a combination of high attention and low activity.

Home Design

B.5 Set up the home environment to accommodate the unique sensory profile

Why?

Changing the environment either by increasing readily available sources of stimulation and/or by decreasing extra stimulation helps to create more opportunities for children and teens to engage calmly. It helps them feel comfortable and more able to focus, which can reduce family battles and daily stress points.

How do we get there?

- Seek professional advice from the therapeutic team on how to adapt your home on the inside and outside to help the child or teen be more successful and less stressed.

- Reduce or remove continual exposure to inputs that are too intense or overstimulating.

- Provide easy access to the sensations that the child or teen seeks and craves (see Kranowitz, 1998).

©Fotosearch Stock Photos

INDIVIDUAL DIFFERENCES

Examples

Increase vestibular and/or proprioceptive: Trampoline, hammock, swings, Lycra trapeze, rubber resistance bands, climbing structure, and occupational therapy–recommended study chairs

Increase tactile: Huge tub of dried beans or dry rice, plastic child's pool for water or bubble play, sandbox, barefoot play, and squishy substances such as playdough

Decrease tactile: Seamless socks, tagless undergarments, soft garments, stretch pants, and long stretch sleeves

Decrease visual: Adjust lighting, simplify or organize the visual field with labeled bins and removal of toys and clutter, and reduce wardrobe/shoe choices

Decrease auditory: Carpeting, drapes, double doors to create sound-dampening airspace barriers, and double-paned windows

Increase oral-motor: Crunchy snacks and crushed ice

Increase taste: Spicy, salty, or sour food

Temperature accommodation: Extra personal cooling or heating devices

Sensory Connections

B.6 Provide daily sensory-motor relational experiences

Why?

Sensory-motor needs provide not-to-be-missed opportunities to strengthen social bonding. By using children's or teens' natural desires for experiencing certain sensations, you can increase their motivation to engage longer and in more complex ways. If you are the provider of the body's sensory needs, you strengthen the child's or teen's attachment to you. Also, if you make sure the body is getting the sensations it is craving every day, then sensory needs are less likely to interrupt other meaningful activity.

How do we get there?

- View sensory-seeking behavior as a clue for how to connect in pleasurable joint activities.

- Suggest daily play based on the sensations the child or teen desires.

- Notice which sensations activate the child or teen for fun playtime and which sensations calm down him or her for achieving focused attention.

- Seize these opportunities to advance relational connection.

©Photodisc

Examples

Tactile seeking: Invite social interaction while immersed in rich tactile resources such as playdough, box of dry beans, sandbox, box of rice, "gooey gook," and so forth.

Body and joint input seeking: Suspend a Lycra trapeze, swing, and cocoons to use for Peekaboo and other engaging interactive play. Take turns pushing each other across the floor in a laundry basket.

Motion seeking: Schedule regular family time on a trampoline; ride together on bicycles or scooters; go sledding or tubing; plan and execute walking, jogging, and hiking training.

Visually distractible: Read together under a tent of blankets with a flashlight.

Balance challenged: Elicit conversations when the child or teen's whole body is supported, such as when he or she is lying on his or her back or in a swimming pool, bean bag chair, or ball pit.

Practice in Play

B.7 Provide daily planned play activities to address processing challenges

Why?

Daily practice in areas of weakness will strengthen children's and teens' overall ability to function at home, school, and community. Learning happens easiest when we are highly engaged and motivated. Use playfulness as the means to help your adolescent or child practice needed microskills.

How do we get there?

- Schedule daily practice sessions using games and environments that elicit the skills that need work.

- When professionals note impairments, ask for and write down ideas for home practice to improve in these areas.

- Keep notes on what works.

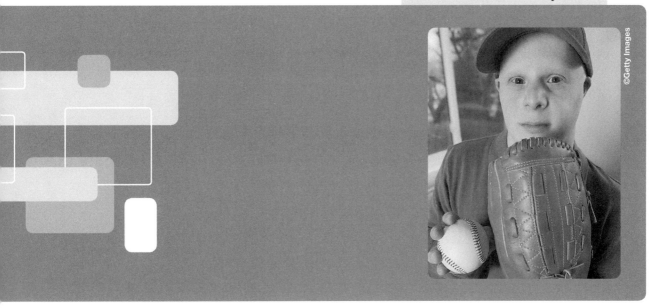

©Getty Images

Examples

Motor planning and sequencing: Together set up an obstacle course that must be navigated to reach the child's or teen's most favorite toys.

Fine motor: Playfully encourage the child or teen to draw simple pictures of what he or she is trying to get you to do in play or daily life. Together cut them out and tape them up around the house as reminders to talk about them.

Social referencing: Play a variation of Hot-Cold Hunt, called Happy-Sad Hunt, with your facial expression as the clues. Play I Spy using only your gaze as a cue.

Gestures and affect: Play Silent Simon Says—the only rule is "no words."

Expressive language: Sing favorite songs together every day in the car—the melody and rhythm of song almost always make speech production and memory retrieval much easier.

Memorization: Small sections of memorization homework on a daily basis work best; repeat, rehearse, and expand gradually.

Regulation and Attention

Attaining a Calm, Alert, Attentive State

The D in DIR® embraces and promotes the stages of human personal development, starting with Capacity 1, Regulation and Attention, or the ability to be calm and alert and to focus. A developmental approach helps children and adolescents attain a calm, alert state before expecting them to achieve further accomplishments in their general developmental trajectory and in any given moment.

Families and professionals tune in and provide needed support for the child or adolescent to achieve regulation and attention. Repeated successes at this sort of relationship-supported regulation extend the child's or teen's eventual capacity to self-regulate and to focus. Research in developmental neurobiology shows the power of caregiver attunement to promote the growth of neural networks and integrated brain systems.

Strategies Include:

ATTUNING—

1.1. **Support regulation:** Help your child or teen get regulated before expecting more.
1.2. **Notice and adjust:** Notice and adjust your intensity to support an optimal arousal level.
1.3. **Calming choices:** Offer choices for help in calming down.
1.4. **Lengthen attention:** Attend to and join interests to expand focus and attention.
1.5. **Avoid flooding:** Support regulation at early stages of upset to avoid emotional "flooding."
1.6. **Practice modulation:** Practice modulation regularly in fun, playful ways.

Support Regulation

Help your child or teen get regulated before expecting more

Why?

Being in a calm, alert state is required before higher capacities can be expressed. In addition, many experiences and memories of adult-supported successful regulation build the child's or teen's ability to be more consistently regulated and eventually help him or her learn to self-regulate.

How do we get there?

- Notice and manage your own regulation states in order to be able to interact calmly.

- Help the child or adolescent reach a calm and alert state before trying to communicate to or expect anything from him or her.

- Help the child or teen learn to read his or her own body signals and cues.

©istockphoto/sonyae

Examples

Preschool/elementary: You are hurrying to get yourself ready and trying to help your son attend to getting dressed for school. He is running in circles and buzzing like a bee; you take this as a cue that he may be alert, but not calm! Using compassion for yourself and for him, calm yourself first with reassuring self-statements. Then provide whatever emotional and physical sensory supports he needs to calm down. Then point to his clothes.

Middle school/high school: You need to remind your adolescent of a chore, but she is focused on the television screen with a glazed expression. You take this as a sign that she may be calm, but not alert! You remember that you need to turn off any electronics before expecting attention, so you give a hand signal warning indicating "5 more minutes" before you are going to turn off the television to talk about the chore plan.

Notice and Adjust

1.2 Notice and adjust your intensity to support an optimal arousal level

Why?

You are the primary tool for helping your child or teen get regulated and engaged. But you must adjust or calibrate this tool, especially your intensity level—that is, how animated or subdued, fast or slow, loud or soft, and challenging or reassuring you are. Once you know what kinds of interactions tend to excite or soothe the child or teen, you can begin to adjust your intensity to support optimal arousal for engagement and learning.

How do we get there?

- Check your own state or level of regulation first: How am I feeling right now? Why?

- Tune in to your child's or teen's state: How calm? How alert?

- Adjust your intensity to the child's or teen's current need for up- or down-regulation.

Examples

Experiment:

- Does it work better for me to match the intensity? Or is it better to go in the opposite direction?

- Should I decrease my volume or tempo?

- Should I increase my emotional expressiveness?

- Should I increase or decrease sensory inputs?

Review video:

- Watch yourself interact or talk with your child or teen.

- Make note of your intensity and modulation.

- Decide which approaches helped the interaction.

- Watch video clips of interactions together with your professional team to get others' input.

Watch yourself live:

- Keep watching yourself in real time as if watching a video.

- Watch your ability to adapt and shift your style to be more effective moment by moment.

Calming Choices

1.3 Offer choices for help in calming down

Why?

Your job is not so much to solve or fix the cause of the upset, but to get through the feelings together. You are working together with your child or teen to arrive at a calmer state, to stay connected through the upset, and to learn more ways for achieving calm. When you take an inquiry approach to young people's upsets, you help them approach upsets in a similar problem-solving way. They become able to reflect on their needs, and they learn to choose from several possible calming strategies. Also, the child or teen remembers the experience of joint emotional problem solving or holds the relational soothing in mind for the future, which builds the foundation for self-calming thoughts and independent self-regulation.

How do we get there?

- Make notes of successful calming strategies from the past.

- Offer just one or two choices at a time so as not to overwhelm.

- Offer choices with few words—do not distract from the task with repetitive or unnecessary words.

- Promote the process of choosing the means for calming.

- Stay open to his or her wishes (if safe and feasible) rather than automatically insisting on your plan.

©istockphoto/Canoneer

Examples

Young child: "Upset?" "Want tummy breathing? Or squeeze hug?"

Middle child: "Do you feel like you need to calm down? Want a blanket sandwich smush? Or want to swing?"

Older child: "You look pretty mad; do you think calling Auntie would help? Or just time to walk around outside in the back?"

Teen: "I can tell you are feeling a little down about it. Remember that sometimes it helps you when you write in your journal, and sometimes it helps when you listen to your 'Chill' playlist…which do you think might help now?"

Lengthen Attention

1.4 Attend to and join interests to expand focus and attention

Why?

A short attention span is a very serious impediment to learning. Obviously, distractibility impairs social connection and academic learning. Children and teens also lose out on opportunities for growth when they spend play time or free time moving aimlessly or repeating actions. Developmental play therapy, or Floortime, does not work on lengthening attention span by force or insistence. Rather, adults join in the natural motivations and interests of children and teens to gradually expand their ability to attend longer to an increasing variety of activities and tasks, including academic projects and extracurricular endeavors.

How do we get there?

* Use your own focused attention as a bridge or scaffolding support to help grow the child's or teen's attention span for purposeful play and meaningful pursuits.

* Experiment to find the games, activities, and materials that are most enticing.

* Watch for clues about what will engage him or her.

* Express genuine interest and enthusiasm for his or her pursuits.

©istockphoto/InkkStudios

ATTUNING

Examples

Preschooler: If his favorite topic or toy is Thomas the Tank Engine, play together with him using Thomas and friends every day to extend his ability to focus and persist at playing purposefully for longer time frames.

Middle schooler: If her favorite sensory activity is flipping the corners of pages in a book, then take trips to the biggest libraries around and show her all of the possibilities. Flip pages with her, and eventually you will find an emerging new interest, perhaps in something inside one of the many books you enjoy together.

High schooler: His pastime is collecting photographs of animals, so open an online account through which to share photos digitally with each other and with others who like the same subject. E-mail him compelling images; help him build an album; post it for others to comment; and invite friends of the family to join, view, and comment.

Avoid Flooding

1.5 Support regulation at early stages of upset to avoid emotional "flooding"

Why?

Regulation is much more attainable from states of mild or moderate agitation than it is from later-stage upset. Step in early to offer emotional attunement and supportive help. If a child or teen has many experiences of collaborating with you to manage upsets, these will provide him or her a sense of emotional competence and therefore more ability to regain calm states going forward. This strategy is not to be confused with habitual attempts to prevent upset; rather, it welcomes opportunities for practice at soothing.

How do we get there?

- Notice early stages of upset or agitation.

- Provide what is needed for support early in the process for success at de-escalating.

- Read subtle cues to know when regulation support is needed.

- Do not fear dysregulation; rather, see the many opportunities for supporting regulation as times to encourage practice and build competence.

Examples

Preverbal child: Notice that she is showing her typical signs of mild frustration about trying to get shoes on. Move closer, offer emotional support with comforting touch, try to simplify the challenge, and offer soothing sensory input if needed.

Verbal child: You might say, "I think you are getting a little upset—do we need to take a break behind the couch? Or outside?"

Nonverbal child or teen: Type on the keyboard (or otherwise appropriately communicate), "Are you feeling frustrated?" The child or teen might type in reply, "Yes." You could type back, "Time to cool down with counting? Or walk outside?" The typed reply might be, "Counting walk."

Practice Modulation

1.6 Practice modulation regularly in fun, playful ways

Why?

Practicing modulation in a fun, playful context helps young people not only practice but also explore, become curious about, and become aware of their own regulation state. If a very active child or teen always hears "calm down" or "slow down," then those modulating reminders become aversive and the child or adolescent starts to tune out the reminders over time. But if offered nonjudgmental invitations to play and think about modulation, the child or teen gets involved in wondering and noticing. If you invite exploration of both ends of the spectrum, it shows that intense isn't necessarily bad. For example, in some celebratory, competitive or, dangerous situations, intensity is required. Then you can move on to show that it is the appropriate modulation of intensity that is important.

How do we get there?

- Choose a calm time to work on these issues so that the interaction does not feel like correction.

- Design games that involve everyone trying varying levels of intensity.

- Eventually add in more shades of gray (low, medium, very strong intensity, etc.).

- Ask questions to invite self-awareness and self-assessment.

- Use what is learned in play and help apply it to daily life challenges.

©Veer/Fancy Photography

Examples

With a group of kids: "Everyone sing the ABC song as fast as you can! Now as slowly as you can. Now medium! Now it's my turn to dance. Was that dance fast, slow, or medium?"

With one child: "Can you talk loud? Talk really soft? How about run very fast?! Run very slowly? Can you give a tight hug? A gentle hug?"

With an older child: "How fast is your motor running right now? How fast was it going when you were at the playground earlier?"

With a preteen: "Pretend you are very excited, as if you're going on stage to play a rock concert. Pretend you are so calm you are falling asleep in class. Pretend you are so fast you can set a world record. Pretend you are so slow you hold up traffic."

Social Engagement

Getting Involved and Connected

Getting involved with, connected to, and attached to people is the most critical capacity in social-emotional development; it is how we grow into members of the human family. DIR® principles show us how to facilitate the development of Capacity 2—children's and adolescents' ability to *connect* with others. First we *observe* them to see what is currently capturing their interest in a particular moment and in general. Then we *harmonize* with their arousal state and sensory needs. Finally, we *join* and become an essential part of their favorite play, conversations, or experiences. This is how we woo them into more robust engagement with ourselves, siblings, and peers—by making social interaction easier or irresistible!

Floortime helps busy families to prioritize *shared pleasure* in each day, making time for parents and children to "fall in love" with each other again. This approach will help an infant, child, or teen grow in his or her capacity to *seek out* and *maintain* engagement with family and friends. Parents are often most concerned about their child's social interaction and success with peers. Using the strategies that follow in this section, parents can also facilitate peer play dates to help their children discover fun in playing together, work out satisfying solutions to conflicts, express emotions productively, and ultimately learn to co-create mutually interesting and pleasurable encounters on their own.

Strategies Include:

CONNECTING—

2.1. **Joint attention:** Develop joint attention.
2.2. **Gaze racking:** Attend to the pattern of gaze.
2.3. **Share pleasure:** Facilitate experiences of mutual joy.
2.4. **Mirror emotions:** Mirror your child's affect by matching facial expression, tone of voice, and tempo.
2.5. **Emphasize affect:** Exaggerate your expression of affect (feeling).
2.6. **Interact:** Turn every action into an interaction.
2.7. **Advance the agenda:** Promote the child's or teen's agenda.
2.8. **Be necessary:** Be the means to an end—be necessary.
2.9. **Use anticipation:** Use anticipation to increase the capacity for mutual attention.

Joint Attention

2.1 | Develop joint attention

Why?

Sharing ideas and experiencing the world of thoughts, sensations, and feelings together form the foundation of meaningful social engagement. Joint attention, or sensing that we both are noticing, thinking about, or feeling the same thing, is what provides a great deal of the sense of pleasure in close relationships. Research shows that joint attention is a key stepping stone to language development, as well. We unconsciously expect others to be able to share attention with us; if it is lacking, we feel uneasy. Your child or teen needs to be comfortable and proficient in joint attention to have successful friendships and partnerships.

How do we get there?

- Watch and join: Follow the child's or adolescent's lead by watching and joining in with his or her rhythm, ideas, interests, and activities.

- Relate eye-to-eye: Adjust your body and the space to promote eye-to-eye interaction. This helps you know what the child or teen is thinking about and feeling. It also helps him or her to remember the pleasure of experiencing the world together with you and to look for your reactions, an experience called *social referencing*. Rather than just facilitating "eye contact," Floortime helps young people develop their interest in looking into others' *minds*.

©istockphoto/dejanristovski

Examples

Children: Start by playing together in mud puddles, with Barbie dolls, or with Pokémon cards. Enter into and try to enjoy just about *whatever* the child's latest fascination may be in order to share an idea and share a feeling!

Teens: Play across from each other or even do academic tasks together face-to-face (not ear-to-ear!) so that you can watch each other and read one another's facial reactions.

Everybody: Use sensory-motor preferences, with touch, sight, sound, motion, and so forth, to enhance joint attention. Once you realize that the shared pleasure is the ultimate goal, developing joint attention can become easier to work into daily routines.

Gaze Tracking

2.2 Attend to the pattern of gaze

Why?

The primary way that children and teens show interest is through their gaze. Watching their gaze is a habit easily developed. It helps you to determine your child's or teen's current interests or intentions, enabling you to follow his or her lead. It is a key way to promote joint attention.

How do we get there?

- Always look at your child's or teen's eyes and follow the gaze to see what her or she is looking at.

- Watch closely to see what brings a gleam to the eye.

- Watch carefully because it may be a very brief glance!

- With more sophisticated preteens or teens, the gaze patterns may be modified and even more subtle, but watch for the subtle changes because the gaze patterns will still reveal interests and emotional reactions.

- Think of the eyes as the windows to thoughts.

©Corbis

CONNECTING

Examples

Lower functioning child: You and your child are playing with cars but you find that he continually looks out the window while aimlessly rolling his car back and forth. As you follow his gaze, you notice the wind blowing the leaves around. Try showing with your actions what you think might be capturing his gaze and attention, for example, swaying your arms with the wind like the trees outside and making wind sounds. At this stage, engagement is a more urgent foundational capacity than is task completion: switching to the child's idea often affords a much better opportunity for supporting his engagement with you or with others.

Higher functioning child: Your child is taking a lot longer than usual to get through the day's homework. Watching her gaze patterns, you notice that she is repeatedly looking all around the page of math problems more than at the one she is working on. You ask, "Are you worried this homework is too long or too hard? Would it help to cover up the other problems so you see only one at a time?"

Teen: When you ask about the school day, he starts looking directly at you when complaining about what you put in his lunch. Rather than getting hurt and defensive, try using the gaze as a sign that this is a topic through which you can really engage together. Ask him, "What snacks would you choose?" "Why do YOU think I put strawberries in for snack?" or "Who should be the lunch maker tomorrow?"

Share Pleasure

2.3 Facilitate experiences of mutual joy

Why?

Deep learning happens in shared states of joy. The more we foster the child's or teen's enjoyment and pleasure, the more he or she will become comfortable with engagement, sustain engagement, and seek out engagement.

How do we get there?

- Look for the gleam in the eye. Always notice what interests, intrigues, motivates, and pleases a child and do more of that—keep it going as long as you can whenever you can.

- Go for joy. Make it your top priority to deepen the warmth and pleasure in the relationship.

- Use pleasant and animated affect throughout play. Use your emotional expression to entice interest and joint attention. This includes using a warm smile, a twinkle in the eye, and a playful tone to woo the child.

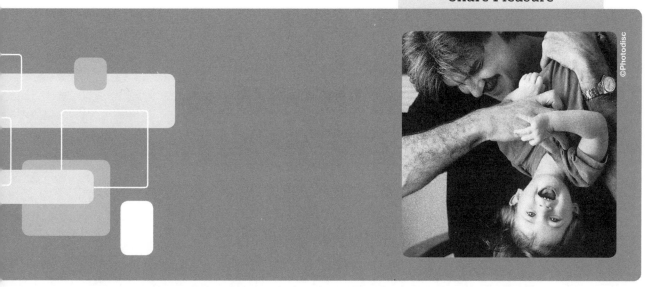

©Photodisc

Examples

Inattentive types: Try silliness—loosen up, shed your inhibitions, and be goofy if that brightens your child's eye.

Movement-seeking types: Try out body games together—chasing and capturing, loud blowing on bellies, rolling down a hill together like logs, and lying on your back and launching the child in the air by balancing him or her on your feet and holding the child's hands.

Auditory-sensitive types: Try *quiet* vocal play—use silly sounds or spontaneous songs, nonsense rhymes, and heated (but whispered) debate on a favorite topic.

Mirror Emotions

Mirror your child's affect by matching facial expression, tone of voice, and tempo

Why?

Mirroring or resonating with a child's or teen's feelings is a tremendously important strategy in the Floortime approach. It helps him or her feel known, understood, and connected to you. Children first learn to know what it is they are feeling by looking into the mirror of empathic reflection by the caregiver. Many infant and child development researchers have demonstrated how this *interactive affective regulation* causes children and adolescents to become relaxed; empathic with others; and able to identify, understand, and manage their own emotions. Interactive affect regulation is the forerunner of self-regulation.

How do we get there?

- Watch the face to pick up expressions and watch the body to see the tone and pace of movement.

- Listen to the tone, pitch, and tempo of vocalizations.

- Match the emotional state by changing your tone, tempo, facial expressions, and even body position to reflect the child's or adolescent's.

- Show that you understand by your words, face, posture, and tone.

©istockphoto/treasurephoto

Examples

Excitement: Join in exuberant play exuberantly.

Anger: Join in joint expressions of frustration. If the first choice of expression violates the "no hurting" rule, then offer safe alternatives first, and wholeheartedly join in.

Sadness: Show a teen or child who is discouraged or down that you feel his or her pain by reflecting this shared emotion in your face, tone, and words.

Emphasize Affect

2.5 Exaggerate your expression of affect (feeling)

Why?

Many children and teens with developmental challenges have trouble noticing or interpreting emotions in others or in themselves. Exaggerating your emotional expressiveness helps them notice and interpret feelings. It also creates a more lively and rich interactive experience that incites and prolongs engagement. In addition, affect-based learning is deep learning because it connects more regions of the brain.

How do we get there?

Show emotional expression in play and daily life through all the senses.

- Vary your facial expressions and responses. Make your emotional reactions obvious and clear. In other words, be easy to read.

- Use vocal gestures (e.g., "uh-oh!," "ohhhh," "ta-da!," "wheee," "oooo") and anticipation (slowly build your volume and tempo).

- Use nonverbal gestures and body movements to emphasize affect, such as clapping, falling down, crouching, running away, and jumping.

- Never exaggerate expressions of true anger or deep sadness. Such expressions could be frightening.

©istockphoto/YanLev

Examples

Confusion: Emphasize a scrunched, questioning face and a helpless-hand gesture.

Mock frustration: When he or she teases you, scowl and stamp your foot.

Joy: Use dramatic wide smiles, happy vocalizations, and celebratory gestures such as claps or thumbs-up signs.

Slight sadness: When your child decides to play by him- or herself, frown and tap on your sad heart.

Interact

2.6 Turn every action into an interaction

Why?

Interaction promotes social development and brain integration. Some children or teens generally prefer to entertain themselves, in which case it may be challenging to know how to start interaction. Greenspan and Wieder (2006) taught parents and clinicians to create opportunities by turning each action into a two-way experience.

How do we get there?

- Memorize the phrase "Turn every action into an interaction" as a guideline or reminder to prioritize the foundational capacity for engagement.

- Use every opportunity to bring self-absorbed or object-focused children into the social arena.

- Teach all members of the family and school team to capitalize on the available time you have together to work on engagement as the bedrock for learning.

©istockphoto/gunnargren

CONNECTING

Examples

Young child: When she is sitting alone, banging on a big ball, see if it captures her attention if you take turns repeating the same rhythm on another ball. Or you can say, "You are the drummer; maybe I can be the *dancer*," and try dancing in a fun or silly way in time to the beat.

Middle child: When kids are working together to build a construction, you can offer to find and organize *all* the pieces and be the "Materials Manager," supplying what they need when they put in their formal requests by pointing, verbalizing, or writing out simple supply requisitions.

Older child: When he asks to play a computer or video game, see if you can make it a joint computer game by saying, "Yes, if I can have the controls and you show me what to click!"

Advance the Agenda

2.7 Promote the child's or teen's agenda

Why?

Noticing and advancing what children or adolescents are aiming to accomplish is a basic joining technique that works beautifully to help you become more salient and more relevant in their world. It requires quieting the agendas in your own mind for the moment, such as academic advancement or development of moral reasoning, and focusing on exactly what they are trying to accomplish. If you are seen as a resource to help make happen what they are trying to do, they will rely on you and turn to you more naturally. This strategy also helps kids and teens feel your acceptance, support, and understanding, which fosters a warm connection with you and leads to stronger self-esteem.

How do we get there?

- Observe first and then join in the effort.

- Set aside your own agendas for the moment if feasible.

- Be the one to help make a child's or teen's idea happen!

- If it is not a safe or wise project, adapt it a bit or suggest an alternative.

- Enrich the project just a little bit to make it even more fun.

Examples

A young child is crawling to hide under a chair—throw a blanket over to make it easier to hide.

An older child is playing in the mud—grab some old clothes for you and for the child to put on, and then bring the hose for more mud-making possibilities.

A preteen is trying to comb his or her hair in a new style—offer a chair and hold a mirror so he or she can have a rear view. Take before and after photos.

A teen boy is planning to invite only female schoolmates to a pool party—help find an appropriate gender mix of friendly peers to invite and help locate their contact information.

Be Necessary

2.8 Be the means to an end—be necessary

Why?

Making yourself necessary is an essential technique for reaching more self-absorbed kids and teens. If you are the means to the end, such as the most fun part of a game, the gatekeeper to highly desired objects and activities, or the one who makes conversation more interesting, then you are fostering social interest and joint attention.

How do we get there?

- Insert yourself into a key role in the enjoyable activity or play.

- Devise games that require your involvement.

- Use child's or teen's particular object focus or sensory focus as clues for how to become necessary.

- Store some toys, books, puzzle pieces, and food in locked or high places that require playful interaction to obtain.

CONNECTING

Examples

Be a part: Your child wants to throw all the balls out of the ball pit one by one, so you might sit blocking the doorway of the ball pit so that you must gather and hand them back one by one, counting the balls together, thus helping the child to throw them again.

Make a part: Create slight challenges that require your help, such as climbing a wall, floating in the deep end of the pool, solving a hard new puzzle, or moving heavy furniture.

Do your part: Your preteen craves lots of sensory input. Rather than resist or discourage this need, *you* be the one to regularly invite and introduce sensory activities that meet a felt need and also require you to play a part, such as a push on the swing, a swim, or a spin around in circles on a chair.

Use Anticipation

2.9 Use anticipation to increase the capacity for mutual attention

Why?

The brain is naturally wired to repeat patterns, to close open-ended problems, and to expect certain outcomes. You can use that natural tendency to capture or sustain a child's or teen's social interest. For example, when you capitalize on the natural motivation to *anticipate* what is coming next and fill in what is missing, he or she will respond to you more consistently. In other words, anticipation draws the child's or teen's attention away from their own inner world into the shared world of your relationship. The more you invite your child to join you by using anticipation, the more likely you will succeed and the longer he or she will remain attentive to you or to a shared activity.

How do we get there?

- Use repetition by repeating familiar, simple games and play routines with a child so he or she learns to anticipate fun with you in predictable ways to boost his or her confidence and joyful engagement.

- Insert pauses into familiar songs, routines, or play expectations to help up-regulate and orient the child's attention.

- Violate expectations in order to elicit more logical responses.

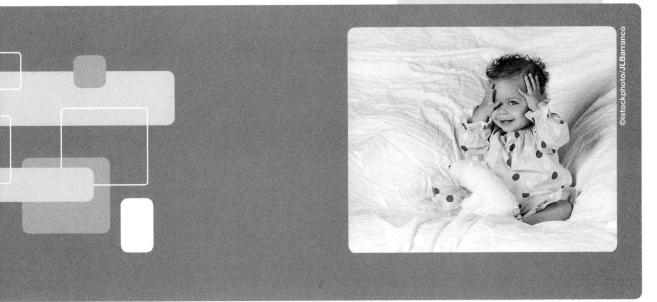

©istockphoto/JLBarranco

Examples

Use repetition: If Peekaboo always elicits a twinkle and a smile, then play Peekaboo every day.

Insert pauses: "Swing up and down, up and down, up and…" "Ready…set… ____!" "Here I come to tickle you, I'm going to find you, I'm getting closer, *here… I…come…*got you! Ahrrrrrrrrrrr!!"

Violate expectations: Put your glasses on upside down. Let your hat fall off your head. Walk into a room backward. Play basketball but cheer each time you miss and pout whenever you make it.

Play routines: With older kids or teens, if playing a certain video game together fosters warm connection during and afterward, play it every day at a planned time in the schedule.

Reciprocal Social Interaction

Initiating and Responding Purposefully

To work on Capacity 3 we focus on helping to develop the essential capacity for social relating: reciprocity, or the give-and-take of human interaction. Developing reciprocity requires continual practice of initiating (opening circles of communication) and responding (closing circles of communication). You can use highly motivating play and joint activities to encourage the child or teen to sustain longer and longer chains of back-and-forth gesturing or verbal dialogue about an idea. Families and professionals must prioritize the fundamental human experience of social *turn taking*, whether through spoken language or alternative forms of communication such as *sign language or typing*. The DIR® approach teaches that it works best to foster turn taking when addressing issues of personal importance and emotional significance to the child or teen. In this way you more easily help him or her to develop purposefulness, initiative, and mutuality.

Strategies Include:

RESPONDING—

3.1. **Invite circles:** Entice to initiate and respond.
3.2. **Total communication:** Do not rely on words alone—use the total communication system.
3.3. **Wait:** Wait long enough for responses to allow for slower auditory, cognitive, and motor-processing speeds.
3.4. **Sportscaster/narrator:** Be the sportscaster/narrator.
3.5. **Playfully persist:** Challenge the child or teen to close follow-up circles.
3.6. **Easy choices:** Offer easy choices if needed.
3.7. **Communication temptation:** Play games requiring initiation.
3.8. **Consider questions:** Carefully craft your questions.

Invite Circles

3.1 Entice to initiate and respond

Why?

Capacity 3 describes back-and-forth reciprocity in verbal and nonverbal dialogue as the hallmark of relating and communicating in warm, connected ways. It is how we fulfill our social nature. Children and teenagers with developmental challenges often have trouble with initiating (opening circles) and responding (closing circles of communication), sometimes one more than the other. Without the capacity to both open and close circles that follow one another in a natural flow, possibilities for interaction are very limited. Furthermore, initiation is the stepping-stone to maturation, competence, and even leadership; responding is the way we take in others and are changed by them.

How do we get there?

- Treat a gesture or a gaze as if it is the opening of a dialogue.

- Respond to whatever the child or teen does.

- Leave pauses! Pauses "pull" for the child to initiate the next circle.

- Always encourage back-and-forth flow as opposed to one-directional conversation.

- Take turns in conversation and play!

- Initiation plus response equals a complete circle.

©istockphoto/Laures

Examples

CHILD:

Open: Your son bangs on the floor with a spoon.

Close: You show an interested reaction on your face, then *wait and watch* to see his facial reaction.

Open: He looks at you with surprise that you are interested.

Close: You give back a surprised look.

Open: You try taking a turn banging.

Close: He giggles at you.

TEEN:

Open: You notice your teen hanging around you, and you look up with expectation.

Close: She says, "Bored."

Open: You ask, "Want to walk the dog? Or help me start dinner?"

Close: She says, "Dog."

Open: You say, "Stay on our street, though."

Close: She scowls at you.

Open: "I know you think you're old enough to walk to Colorado, but the rule is …" You pause.

Close: She smirks and says, "Stay on our street!"

Total Communication

3.2 Do not rely on words alone—use the total communication system

Why?

Human communication combines verbal and nonverbal expression. It relies on so-called "left-brain" orderly decoding and "right-brain" holistic comprehension. Utilizing a variety of verbal and nonverbal communication techniques engages both sides of the brain and integrates them. This integrated communication deepens and broadens a child's or teen's ability to express and comprehend literal meaning and emotional meaning. When thinking about your child's or teen's language development, avoid the mistake of thinking of it as the acquisition of practiced words or phrases. Rather, understand that all language is social in nature and that language development rests on a crucial bedrock of holistic social comprehension.

How do we get there?

- Combine words, affect, and action for best results. Use music and rhythmic motor integration activities to improve responsive timing.

- Use facial expressions, hand gestures, vocal tone, and body language to help get across the full meaning of your communication.

- Use facial expressions and body language to accentuate the emotion in what you say and do.

- Play games that rely only on body language to help you and your child focus on other systems of communication.

- To enhance your awareness of the total communication system, practice foregoing words in favor of other forms of communication for 20-minute increments.

Examples

Child with severe challenges: When she runs from you, use large gestures and increased affect, "I'mmm … gonnnnna … *get you!*" After you "capture" her, step back, pause, and use a big, slow shrug before saying with a puzzled look and hand gesture, "*Now* what?"

Child with moderate challenges: Try building a castle with sand or blocks or a train track using only gestures and sounds. Videotape yourself during this attempt to watch, laugh, and learn.

Child or preteen with mild challenges: Play board games, card games, parlor games, or playground games using only gestures for fun and for practice in reading and sending signals. Vary this by playing in teams and having the teams confer to figure out what the other side is trying to communicate.

Wait

3.3 Wait long enough for responses in order to allow for slower auditory, cognitive, and motor-processing speeds

Why?

Many children with developmental differences take extra time to take in and make sense of stimuli as well as more time to plan and execute a verbal or nonverbal response. The expected wait time for human beings to respond is an unconscious expectation, therefore it takes care and intentional practice to learn to alter that expectation and wait long enough. Waiting long enough opens up the opportunity for true reciprocal communication and lays a groundwork for the child's initiation. By waiting you are giving your child time to start an interaction or respond to what you've said or done and to achieve *interactive synchrony*.

How do we get there?

- Assume that the child has an idea or a response.

- Pause for plenty of time for your child or teen to process (interpret) the information at hand and plenty of time for him or her to plan and produce the gesture, expression, or verbal communication.

- Maintain your gesture and facial expression while waiting to encourage a response and show that you are waiting.

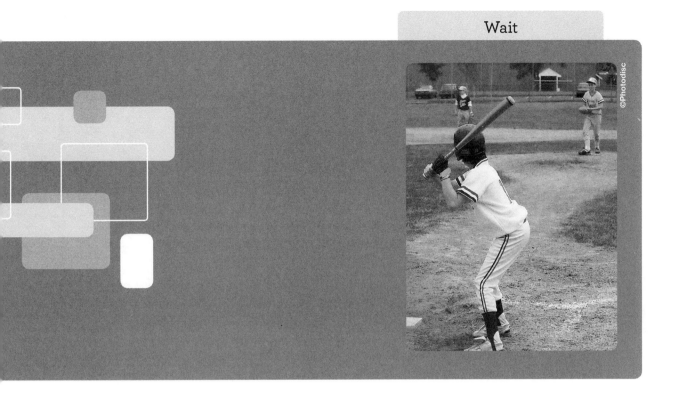

Wait

©Photodisc

Examples

Mom, dad, or grandparent: The doorbell rings. Try just looking at the young person with an expectant expression and don't rush him in his response. This gives him a chance to initiate a communication about someone being at the door or about answering the door.

Nanny: "Do you want your frozen yogurt in a cup or cone?" Perhaps the child replies, "Cone!" Now wait with expectation for her to initiate the next dialogue circle. Gently touch her shoulder, chin, or lips if physical cues help her with initiation of a communication turn.

Teacher, tutor, or one-to-one aide: When you have a student with slower processing speed, be sure to let him or her know ahead of time that you will be asking for an answer and then give the student time to offer a response rather than only giving those who are first with an answer a chance to participate. Help the others in class work further on the problem while they wait for slower students to formulate responses.

Sportscaster/ Narrator

3.4 Be the sportscaster/narrator

Why?

Support the child's capacity for dialogue, reciprocity, and purposefulness by narrating everything you see happening in the child's play. It might seem simple or unimpressive; however, narrating is one of the more powerful Floortime strategies. When you describe what you see children or teens trying to do, it helps them feel noticed, accepted, and cared for. This enhances self-esteem, but it also clarifies their intentions and raises their self-awareness. Increasing self-awareness of their actions and intentions contributes to the development of purposefulness, or more thoughtful intentionality.

How do we get there?

- Watch what the infant, toddler, child, or teen does and guess what he or she may be thinking.

- Briefly and simply keep up a natural flow of commentary to communicate your interest, comprehension, and general acceptance of his or her thoughts and ideas.

- Put his or her possible thoughts into words.

- Use narration as a bridge when dialogue is not flowing.

- Avoid directing the action or evaluating it—just describe it.

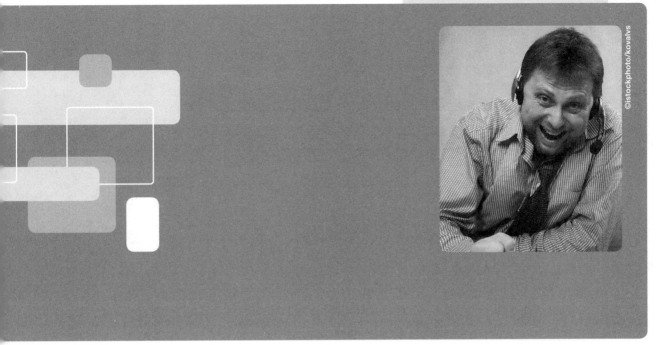

Examples

With a preschooler: "Okay, you've got the bus, and all the beads are going in the bus. Oops, you found one more bead under your bed. Now you have all the beads. Ahh—they all fit!"

With an elementary schooler: "Ah, you crawled behind the couch so I couldn't get you with my sword anymore—now you're safe!"

With a junior high schooler: "Okay, I see. You drew the logo again, but you made it really tiny this time."

Playfully Persist

3.5 Challenge the child or teen to close follow-up circles

Why?

Playfully persisting in communication endeavors means you challenge a young person to close circles consistently with other people. Persistence is one way you encourage "full circle" communication. When you hang in there and don't settle for interactions in short bits and bytes, it shows children or adolescents that you are genuinely interested in what they think or how they feel. It also supports their belief that their response and input are important. Forcing interaction will not engender the positive affect to help learning, but playful persistence sets up an expectation that interaction is not a stop/start endeavor but rather a continuous sharing of ideas.

How do we get there?

- If the child or teen doesn't respond, persist at getting a reply, but be sure to use a playful manner.

- If he or she responds by saying or doing something unrelated, playfully use it as a response to your question.

- You can end your efforts when you are convinced playfulness is not enticing a response this time, satisfied that you are establishing a pattern of expectation of interaction that flows.

- You can let the child or teen get to know more about your internal states at this stage, so you may express your eagerness to hear a response or disappointment when reciprocal communication is interrupted.

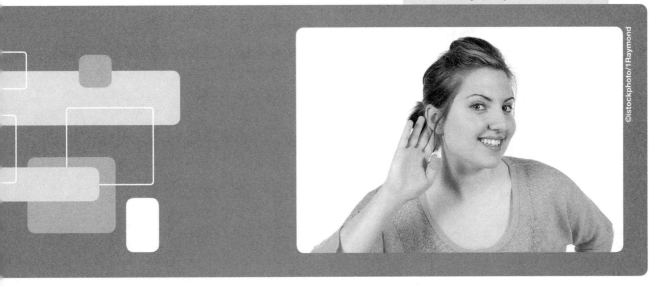

©istockphoto/1 Raymond

Examples

In school: The one-to-one aide asks her student what he might say to the teacher's open-ended question about the reading assignment. The student looks as if he hasn't heard the aide, so the aide kneels down, gets a bit closer, places her hand on the student's shoulder, says "I really want to know what you think," and invites the student to think with her about the question.

At home: Playing with toy cars, you drive yours close and ask her car, "Hi, where are you going?" She does not answer, so you shrug with your hands up and wear a questioning look on your face. She looks away, and you say, "Oh! Over there?!" and move the car in the direction of her gaze. Then ask again in a new way.

At the park: You are talking together about the leaves changing color. You ask what color he sees, and he responds impulsively with his favorite color: "Blue!" You show surprise, then tie it in to the conversation about leaves and say, "Blue leaves?! Uh-oh, the tree is sick?!" Wait for him to fix this or to close the circle and continue the conversation.

Easy Choices

3.6 Offer easy choices if needed

Why?

Choosing between two choices is much easier than responding to open-ended questions. Choosing between an appropriate answer and a silly answer is even easier. With the goal of rapid back-and-forth exchange, make it easy. Give lots of opportunities for the child or teen to respond and close the circle. Silly choices will increase lightheartedness in your interactions as well, which is important even though the goals and aims of this sort of work are weighty.

How do we get there?

- Offer open-ended questions at first. If the child does not respond, offer two choices of answers.

- To add playfulness or to make the choice easier at first, make one of the choices ridiculous.

Easy Choices

©istockphoto/davidmody

Examples

Your child: When deciding what to do next, she hesitates, so you support the continuing exchange by asking, "What should we play next?" You wait but she does not respond. You offer, "Should we play dominoes, or clean your room?"

Your student: At break time, he doesn't initiate a choice but just sits at his desk. You write two potential free time choices on his white board: "swings" and "math problems." He points to swings and gets up to go outside.

Your therapy client: She is having a hard time explaining what made her angry at her mother so you give two choices, one logical and one very unlikely (making it easy to rule out). You ask, "Is it maybe that you didn't want your mom to say you had to finish all your homework tonight? Or that you didn't want her to make dinner?"

Communication Temptation

3.7 Play games requiring initiation

Why?

Very often children and adolescents with special needs get used to being told what to do all day long. They become dependent on instructions and may be slow to develop initiative and social assertiveness. Helping children and adolescents learn to put their ideas into words and to initiate communication is tough—they need extra motivation to practice this continuously. Games that are devised to provide "communication temptations" are effective in enticing the child to practice opening many circles in a row without a battle over compliance.

How do we get there?

- Incorporate communication temptations into daily routines.

- Incorporate communication temptations into indoor and outdoor play together.

- Expect communication in every encounter.

- Expect/anticipate/wait for the child or teen to initiate.

Communication Temptation

©istockphoto/vgajic

Examples

With a younger child, play piggyback, but don't move without directions from the child on where to go and how to go (fast/slow, bumpy/smooth, straight/curvy). Play computer or video games only if *you* get to control the mouse or the game controller and the child directs you regarding what you must click.

With an older child, blindfold yourself and have the child direct you by voice to a favorite toy (you might provide a pretend microphone, megaphone, or headset mic to encourage the voice commands).

Consider Questions

3.8 Carefully craft your questions

Why?

When children or adolescents tend to be uncertain or reticent in communication, adults often fill in the blanks with a series of closed-ended questions. Too many questions to process can be distressing and potentially dysregulating. Closed-ended questions encourage one-directional communication from adult to child and may squelch reciprocal conversation. Instead, craft questions carefully and use sparingly. Choosing appropriately challenging questions increases the chances of your child or teen understanding and responding.

How do we get there?

Think about *how many* and *what kind* of questions you ask, keeping in mind how ready the child or teen is to understand them and respond (Feder, 2008).

- How many: Limit your ratio of questions to 20%—the rest of the time use comments, sentence stems, and narration.

- What kind: Open-ended questions encourage more thought; multiple-choice questions make responding easier; and targeted or specific questions may encourage more responsiveness.

- How ready: Ensure developmental readiness for *wh* questions. *What, where, when*, and *who* questions are easier to respond to than *how* and *why* questions.

Examples

Multiple choice: Did you like circle time or recess best?

Targeted: Who did you play with at school today?

Comment: You look like you had a hard day.

Sentence stem: When we get home, let's play _____.

Open ended: Why do you think he said that to her?

Complex Communication

Using Gestures and Words to Solve Problems Together

Capacity 4 is a major developmental threshold that you can help your child or teenager cross. DIRFloortime® methods are designed to move a child or teen from engaging in "islands" or isolated moments of reciprocity to being able to sustain a continuous flow of rapid, back-and-forth emotional communication exchanges. More sustained and sophisticated communication is critical for success in meaningful and satisfying relationships. A young person at Capacity 3 may open or close up to 10 circles in a row; when working on Capacity 4 we aim to *expand* interactions to more than 50 dialogue circles in a row on the same topic.

At this stage, young people begin to develop a *sense of self* and a clearer concept of *the other*. This is what allows for the initial development of *theory of mind*, or the understanding of others' mental states and perspectives. Even more wonderful, it allows for *intersubjectivity*, or the delightful *awareness* of joining, aligning, resonating, sharing, and knowing/being known. At this stage, you may negotiate playfully and express your perspectives and feelings and incorporate these into the experience of being together. As a young person *expands* his or her continuous mental picture of self and other, he or she becomes capable of more organized, goal-directed sequences of personal and social behavior.

Strategies Include:

EXPANDING—

4.1. **Stretch interactions:** Stretch out interaction chains to 50 or more circles in a row.

4.2. **Don't judge:** Express interest in all attempts to communicate.

4.3. **Feign ignorance:** Expand reciprocal communication by pretending to be ignorant.

4.4. **Assign meaning:** Treat all play actions as if they are goal directed.

4.5. **Playfully obstruct:** Use playful obstruction to expand interactions and encourage joint problem solving.

4.6. **Devise problems:** Set up the environment to promote independent problem solving.

4.7. **Genuine self:** Allow more of your genuine self in interactions.

4.8. **Social flow:** Enhance understanding of emotional meaning and flow of social interactions.

Stretch Interactions

4.1 Stretch out interaction chains to 50 or more circles in a row

Why?

Here you are working to help a teen or a child become able to have sustained conversations by capitalizing on almost every interaction and drawing it out. Having sustained conversations with many communication turns flowing rapidly between people helps us understand other people and ourselves in relationship; it also allows us to adapt ourselves to others to achieve social harmony in a pleasurable sense of "getting along" with or achieving our interpersonal goals with others. It is how human beings build intimacy, understanding, and even polite assertiveness. Social flow is a kingpin capacity.

How do we get there?

- Expand and develop any topic of conversation or play, whether frivolous or serious.

- Encourage negotiation rather than compliance at this crucial stage.

- Make longer flow of interactions the most important goal for now.

- Take the *least efficient* route in a conversation to stretch conversations out.

- Avoid stopping at yes/no, closed-ended questions—keep the flow going.

©Photodisc

Examples

With a preschool child: Be silly or playful even in routine, daily tasks to stretch them out. Instead of asking, "Did you brush your teeth?" offer to be a fortune teller guessing which teeth got brushed: "Did you brush that tooth?" Point to one, allow time for a response, then you could follow up with, "What about that tooth?" "Did you brush your nose, too?"

With an adolescent: Stephen asks if he may pop some popcorn instead of eating the prepared dinner. Instead of giving a simple, authoritative answer, Dad invites interaction with more provocative responses, like "How come you want to make your own?", "How about you make popcorn for everybody?", "Let's plan how you could get the nutrition you need tonight…", and "What makes popcorn better than chicken fingers?"

With a school-age child: You can stretch out even the simplest conversation:

- "You want a drink? Okay, what kind of drink?"

- "In which kind of cup?"

- "Okay. Why is that one your favorite?"

- "What temperature?"

- "How much?"

Don't Judge

4.2 Express interest in all attempts to communicate

Why?

You may expand and elaborate children's and adolescents' communications by working with any comments or ideas they initiate. Taking genuine interest in their natural motivation to share an idea, even if it is mistaken, odd, repetitive, or even insensitive, is the most likely method to deepen or stretch their understanding of others and support rich communication with others.

How do we get there?

- Accept any and all attempts to communicate as legitimate communications at this stage.

- Don't judge correctness of ideas or topic choice when working on this capacity.

- Identify with your child's or teen's feelings of being intensely interested in something so that you are able to express genuine (not fake) interest in preferred topics.

- Express curiosity.

- Follow up on any communication to keep the ideas flowing.

©istockphoto/XiXinXing

Examples

With a young child: He laughs and points at squash on the plate and says, "Poo poo." Postpone manners lessons until the child has mastered this crucial Capacity 4. Instead, engage the conversation playfully by saying something like, "Poo poo?! Yuck!" The child might laugh and say, "Doggy poo poo." You could take a bite and say, "MMM, good doggy poo poo." (Plus, if you connect in this warm, satisfying way, your manners lessons will be adopted more wholeheartedly.)

With an older child: She announces she is going to get rich by selling lemonade and sodas every day after school. Forego the economics lesson and the feasibility critique; don't judge opinions and ideas. Rather, try saying something such as the following: "Ooooh, you are determined" and "How much will you charge?"

With a preteen: He is upset and asks you to go away. Instead of taking offense or correcting the insensitivity at this critical stage of encouraging communication flow, instead be curious; "You want me to go away?" "How far should I go?" "Will that help you feel better?" "Do you think you will want me to come back?"

Feign Ignorance

4.3 Expand reciprocal communication by pretending to be ignorant

Why?

Children often experience their caregivers as fairly omnipotent. For this reason, feigning ignorance provokes or entices communication in an irresistible fashion. Younger people who see the need to direct or correct older people are enticed to communicate in longer sequences of interaction. They are also solidifying their grasp of information that they do know by explaining it to the adult who obviously needs some information.

How do we get there?

- Misunderstand playfully.

- Have trouble in your task.

- Offer several options for a solution if the child gets stuck offering you help.

- Monitor your child's or teen's responses as you go, and modify yours accordingly.

- Use this strategy sparingly and always make it fun and playful, rather than frustrating.

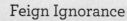

Feign Ignorance

©Photodisc

Examples

- Respond to requests for retrieving food on high shelves or hard-to-get places in a slightly confused way, indicating you require some coaching from the child.

- Do something a little bit wrong (e.g., drive a toy car upside down).

- Have trouble figuring out a physical challenge. ("I'm stuck!")

- Pretend you can't get something open. (Mutter, "Uunnhh!")

- Let your teen explain things to you. ("How does fantasy football work?")

Assign Meaning

4.4 Treat all play actions as if they are goal directed

Why?

Some children and teens have intermittent periods of seemingly aimless activity. Sometimes it is repetitive or habitual. Treating each behavior as if it is purposeful is one way to determine the young peoples' hidden purposes; if you are wrong, they are likely to show you what their purpose was! If it is indeed mere aimless activity, treating it as if it is meaningful is the best way to kick-start the child into thinking more intentionally about choosing behaviors. In other words, assuming meaningfulness is one way to foster the intentionality, goal direction, purposefulness, and behavioral organization that make up Capacity 4.

How do we get there?

- Try to imagine the child's *possible* basic purpose or intention.

- Play out the possibility.

- Find a purpose! Even when it does not seem like children or adolescents are engaged in purposeful play, try finding one—help them be purposeful and create meaning where none may appear to exist.

Examples

Younger child: As she is lining up play food items, you can say, "Oh, I see, we have 1, 2, 3, 4, 5...6 things to eat today!" If that doesn't seem to sink in, you can try pointing and say, "This is how we cook? First burger, then pickles, then potato? That'll work!"

Older child: If she is lining up cars, you can say, "Oh, you put all the cars together. You made a car showroom! Let's look for the one you want to buy."

Teen: If she won't throw away any of her stacks of magazines in her room, you could assume purposefulness in this way: "Maybe you want a complete collection? We could organize them by date and arrange them on shelves. Or we could check on eBay to see if you could bid on vintage issues at a reasonable price."

Any age: When your son starts climbing over the back of the couch, you can say, "Okay, *you're* going to hide from *me* this time!" When he walks away from a game in the middle of it, you can ask, "Oh, time for something new? All done?"

Playfully Obstruct

4.5 Use playful obstruction to expand interactions and encourage joint problem solving

Why?

Playful obstruction means finding a way to *playfully* thwart the child's or teen's activity so that he or she has to interact with you to meet his or her goal. In other words, you create a fun social problem to be solved. When done sensitively, this technique both instigates longer chains of complex communication for solving the social problem and supports behavioral organization through persistence at purposeful, goal-directed activity.

How do we get there?

- Playfully insert problems that need to be solved into the play path or routines.

- Don't forget the *playful* part of this; it's the key!

- Don't stop your empathy when you become a bit provoking; stay attuned and connected.

- Stay playful by winking, flashing a smile, or casting a playful glance.

- Follow the child's or teen's lead on whether and how frequently he or she can manage some playful obstruction and *still have fun with you*.

- Use this strategy *sparingly* so that you don't disrupt the attuned, warm connection you have established.

©istockphoto/tomasworks

Examples

Add a challenge: "What if I can't reach the cereal you want?"

Be like Detective Colombo: You can be the skeptical detective: "But wait a minute, ma'am, you just told me your story but just one thing doesn't seem quite right here—I think YOU are the guilty one!"

Throw a monkey wrench: Playfully get in the path, cover a toy, or hide a desired object enticingly behind your back.

Complicate: "Okay, the bus can head over to the school, but can it stop so that the kids can get breakfast *first?* They're very *hungry!*"

Devise Problems

4.6 Set up the environment to promote independent problem solving

Why?

Thinking for oneself requires practice, practice, and more practice. Therefore, as adults, we must work ourselves out of the role of solving problems and doing everything for younger people in our care. Instead, in order to provide sufficient practice, we must set up environments rich in problems for children or adolescents to solve together or independently. Solving motor planning challenges, logical problems, and social problems paves the way for purposefulness and successful adaptation to the social and work worlds. Proposing and instigating solvable problems in the environment is the best sort of preparation for the future.

How do we get there?

- Create problems to solve in the physical play environment (obstacle courses, play boxing).

- Create solvable problems in play, conversation, or daily routines.

- Make wrong moves that call for correction and help from the child or teen.

- Solve problems together.

- Leave room for the child's ideas or solutions to form; be patient.

- Encourage brainstorming—invite and entertain all possible solutions.

- Don't discourage any attempted solutions—don't criticize or judge.

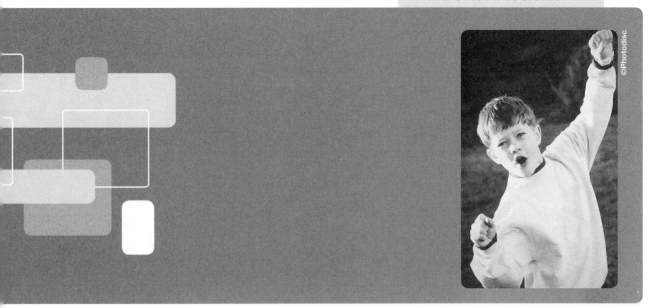

Examples

Interaction at home: Your daughter drops her glove while walking from the house to the car. Don't bend down and pick it up or give her a command to do so— wait until she notices one glove missing, then show expressions on your face of surprise and quizzical wondering, and, if needed, point slowly in the direction from which she came.

Routines at school: Rather than directing a student through the morning routine, ask, "What's next?" Point to the clock, a picture schedule, or a written schedule if needed. Have the student direct you through a familiar routine as well.

Recreation in the community: When riding bikes to the local park, bike trail, or store, let your child plan the route, with you only offering help if asked or if needed for safety and feasibility of the trip.

Genuine Self

Allow more of your
genuine self in interactions

Why?

At this stage of growth, young people are working to develop a sense of the *other person*. Some need to learn what others feel, while many need to learn to *remember* to think about what others may feel. Even more basic is the difficult discovery that people to whom we are close do not always feel the same as we do or want things to be the way that we do. Expressing some of your own ideas and feelings helps children and teens build a more complete sense of your internal reality and helps them develop a better perspective on others in general. Also, when you add your will, perspectives, and feelings into the relationship gradually, it helps prepare the child or teen for more successful peer interactions.

How do we get there?

- Alternate turns about who makes the next plan for play or activity choice—with preparation and visual cues such as a written order of turns, children can often tolerate waiting for their turn.

- Express occasional gentle reluctance to go along with the child's or the teen's activity or play idea if you sense he or she can still remain engaged.

- Don't overwhelm with heavy feelings; provide a *tolerable* amount of play-relevant emotion.

- Communicate clear limits on acceptable versus nonacceptable behavior.

EXPANDING

©Image Source

Examples

Toddler: "I feel sad if you always pick your favorite book and not mine."

Preschooler: "Hey, I want to crack an egg, too! May I have a turn next, and then you have a turn after that?"

Elementary: "It's not okay with friends to scream when you are upset; it makes them scared. Also, it may make kids think that you don't like them."

Preteen: "No hurting anyone, or we will have to stop wrestling for today."

Teen: "I was really looking forward to talking together while we walk. Remember the rule that we use only one ear bud when we are with people?"

Social Flow

4.8 Enhance understanding of emotional meaning and flow of social interactions

Why?

To understand and succeed in the social world, the child or teen must be able to understand and participate in the flow of verbal and nonverbal emotional communication as it develops and changes. Developing this capacity takes a lot of practice and may require much support. You can serve as a "translator" to explain what the child or teen might have missed in social interactions, and you can be a guide to support him or her to develop better flow with peers or family members.

How do we get there?

- *Engage* in long chains of interaction around your child's interests.

- At first, *focus* more on nonverbal back-and-forth trading of signals rather than verbal conversation. Engage in a series of interactive emotional signals or gestures to communicate.

- *Narrate* or describe the details of what is happening in social situations in real life, television, or books.

- *Fill in* by explaining what may be assumed and what may be a nuance of meaning.

- *Check in* with your child's or teen's social comprehension and fill in the gaps of his or her understanding as necessary.

- *Write* a Social Story (Gray, 2010) that explains a hard-to-learn social reality.

©Photodisc

Examples

Body awareness: Play the copycat game. Have two children or teens copy one another's sounds, gestures, funny faces, body movements, dance steps, and so forth.

Social awareness: Support interaction with a peer. Say, "See his eyes on you? He's waiting for you to decide. Remember he said he was hoping you would say yes to playing ball?"

Social meaning: Tell the child or teen, "If he's winking and half-smiling, it looks like he is using some sarcasm to be playful and make you laugh."

Social Story: Have the child or teen write a short, simple story that reassures him or her and explains the meaning of a social reality, such as, "Five Ways to Join People on the Playground."

Symbolic Play

Creating and Using Ideas

Creating ideas and using symbols represent the fifth rung on the DIR® social-emotional developmental ladder. Capacity 5 describes an essential step up in a child's or teen's development, one that is critical to the full expression of humanity. Using symbols in pretend play and other imaginative endeavors allows us to reflect on reality in a variety of ways and to think of new abstract possibilities—to hypothesize, to imagine, and to use what we have experienced in new ways that go beyond our concrete experience and enlighten us. For these reasons, DIRFloortime® places high importance on playing with a child every day using toy characters or whole-body role playing.

With teens, symbolic play may take various forms, such as writing stories or plays together, creating videos, imagining alternate film endings, and so forth. Supporting children and teens in symbolic interaction with adults as well as with other young people helps them develop a rich imaginative life, creativity, abstract thinking, and high-level social cooperation. Parents and professionals can promote this capacity by entering the young peoples' imaginative narratives and expanding the breadth and depth of ideas and emotional content. This often takes place through the imaginative act of *pretending*.

Strategies Include:

PRETENDING—

5.1. **Use pretend:** Create opportunities for pretending.
5.2. **Animate:** Bring the characters to life.
5.3. **Thicken the plot:** Deepen the plot and add complexity.
5.4. **Instigate creativity:** Expand the opportunities for creativity.
5.5. **Vary emotions:** Broaden the emotional themes.
5.6. **Challenge and support:** Take on dual roles within play.
5.7. **Enrich play:** Vary the forms of symbolic play.

Use Pretend

5.1 Create opportunities for pretending

Why?

Look to create opportunities in play and daily life to encourage and draw out the imagination of your child or adolescent. Humans' ability to form new ideas develops first through play that goes beyond simple imitation to the initiation of brand new combinations of actions and ideas. Along with this idea-laden play comes the expanded use of words. Through representational play and expanded use of words, young people are learning to use sounds and objects to stand for ideas. This opens up the world of higher order thought. Symbols allow young people to manipulate ideas or to use them in ways that result in new creations, new solutions, or inventions.

How do we get there?

- Don't always rely on structured forms of play like puzzles, books, board games, or organized sports and playground games.

- Choose materials or spaces that invite creativity and leave room for spontaneity.

- Get yourself into the child's or teen's space and take on a character—such as a bear or wizard—in a pretend drama of the child's own choosing.

- Ham it up! Interact, talk, and emote through your character. Don't worry if you're putting on a good performance; the point is to be animated and playful.

©Veer/Fancy Photography

PRETENDING

Examples

Animate: If a student is randomly pushing a train around the track, you might get a toy, put it on the train, and say in a character voice, "I want a ride." Or you may talk as if you are the train moving its cargo.

Create: Give symbolic meaning to objects as you play. If he climbs to the top of the sofa, pretend he is climbing a tall mountain. If she goes down the slide at the playground, pretend she is sliding into the ocean and help her watch out for the fish.

Dramatize: Take on roles and together act out stories or videos that your child or teen enjoys; try to enlist others to join.

Recreate: With your preteen or teen, you can role-play real situations to imagine how to manage them, work to improve the plot of a book or film, design improvements to a digital game, or draw an entirely new game.

Animate

5.2 Bring the characters to life

Why?

When you bring objects and toy characters to life by giving them a voice and a perspective, you immediately add imaginative, pretend, or symbolic thinking to the encounter. Animating characters, or pretending they are alive, helps young people join you in play as a pretend character rather than just as a director or an audience member. They gain a much richer experience of a pretend play situation when the characters are imagined to be living, breathing, talking, and feeling beings.

How do we get there?

- Animate the characters (bring them to life) by speaking from their perspective.

- Try using a voice that sounds quite different in pitch or accent from your own to distinguish the character from yourself and to help a character seem to come to life. (Don't worry about being "good" at it—often a really bad impersonation can instigate more fun and communication.)

- Hold up the toy or image of the character that you are pretending to be, look at the figure when it is "talking," and give it lifelike movement.

Animate

©istockphoto/yaruta

Examples

Impersonate: Do your best impression! Talk like Mickey, Yoda, or whichever character you are playing. If your daughter is playing with a stuffed animal, use another animal to talk with hers. Have your character actually fly through the air and jump from building to building as he talks.

Invite: If your child is directing the play and not joining as a character, say, "I'm going to be the ambulance driver; are you going to be the police?" Or use your character to speak to one of the toys the child is holding and then pause to wait for an answer: "Hey, Frog, what do you want to eat for breakfast?"

Channel: Even your teen may appreciate your trying this: have him or her help you speak for an iPad or backpack, figuring out what these familiar items might say. Or you might ask him or her to act out what friends or teachers typically say and how they say it.

Thicken the Plot

5.3 | Deepen the plot and add complexity

Why?

Playing is an embodied way of thinking. Playing with complex ideas facilitates learning to think at a higher level. Some children and adolescents with developmental challenges get stalled at concrete levels of play or ideation. It is up to attuned adults around them to help move them over the bridge to richer ideas, and then they definitely can fly with them.

How do we get there?

- Complicate: Summarize the drama and ask for clarification or present a twist to the plot to make it more intriguing to your child.

- Elaborate: Patiently play along with enjoyable scenarios for a while to connect, then gradually introduce a slight change.

- Delineate: Help your child and teen create a beginning, middle, and end to their stories by summarizing the drama and asking about what happens next.

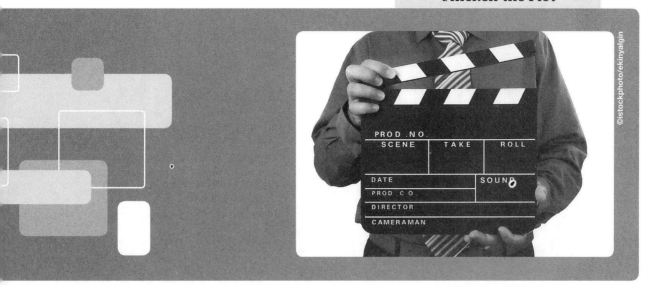

Examples

Elaborate: "Oh, I see, okay, we're in a rocket ship! So should I call you Captain _____ (child's name)?"

Complicate: "All right, here we go to the moon again! We're *almost* there. I can see craters. Oh no, we're almost out of fuel!"

Delineate: "So first the aliens came, and then the townspeople joined forces. What's going to happen at the end?"

Instigate Creativity

5.4 Expand the opportunities for creativity

Why?

We need to take young people at Capacity 5 as far as possible into creating more ideas and more complex ideas. If they can learn to let their imaginations run wild, they can be flexible with others and flexibly solve problems.

How do we get there?

- Use the mishaps: Upsets in play can be used to generate more creativity.

- Turn up the silliness: To encourage playfulness and creativity, be goofy. It shows that there is no right or wrong during pretend play.

- Perform: Help stage a puppet show, circus, Olympics, concert, or a play.

Examples

The mishaps: If she gets stuck in zippered clothing, you can try suggesting it was maybe her favorite bad-guy character's trap; plan together how to make a worse trap for the bad guy.

The silliness: "No more forks ever! We'll eat this spaghetti straight from the bowl! No more napkins, either." Or "I'm the tickle monster sent special delivery to … *you!*"

The performance: Make tickets, plan a performance, rehearse the song or dramatic skit, set up chairs, and invite the rest of the family or neighbor friends to watch.

Vary Emotions

5.5 Broaden the emotional themes

Why?

Greenspan and Wieder (1998) repeatedly stressed the importance of playing with a wide variety of emotional themes in imaginative play. This helps children expand their emotional range in a safe environment and sets the stage for the next rung on the ladder, which involves emotional thinking. In other words, emotional playing comes before emotional thinking. Children and adolescents with developmental challenges often feel comfortable with a familiar, small range of emotions and may feel less comfortable than others do about exploring certain challenging emotions. Play and imagination can entice them to broaden their comfort zone.

How do we get there?

Explore the gamut by using the following themes in play:

- Nurturance and dependence
- Pleasure and excitement
- Curiosity
- Power and assertiveness
- Anger and aggression
- Limit setting
- Fears and anxieties
- Disgust
- Desire
- Sadness
- Pride and competence
- Love
- Control
- Envy
- Shame and embarrassment
- Rejection and loneliness
- Confusion
- Admiration and adoration

Examples

Joy and happiness: Reenacting celebrations and high points in life such as class trips, birthdays, family trips, and so forth can help reinforce awareness of positive emotions.

Anger and aggression: Playing about aggression is a safe and acceptable way to express this impulse. Don't negate it! When your child's character grabs your own character's toy, you may rant and rave, for example, saying simply, "No! No! No! Angry, angry, angry!" Make it clear you are comfortable with anger, so your child can be too.

Limit setting: Sometimes children and teens need to exert a sense of control over their world by taking turns playing at being the ones who are setting limits, that is, putting bad guys in jail, making dolls go to bed early, and so forth.

Rejection or embarrassment: Young peoples' worry about being weird, being laughed at, or being excluded can feel unmentionable, but it may be introduced by your character in play. Including these difficult themes in a teen's story writing can be cathartic.

Challenge and Support

5.6 Take on dual roles within play

Why?

Using dual roles allows one adult to take on both a familiar, safe role in the play and a more challenging role at the same time. This creates a safe space for the child or teen to interact with a challenging persona. When you take on two personas, the child or teen can move out of all-or-nothing, black-and-white, concrete thinking—for example, you can be the good guy and the bad guy at the same time.

How do we get there?

- Play a dual role of supporting your child's or teen's ideas as an ally but presenting opposition or challenge to the idea at hand.

- Create a problem. Then, speaking as a character, challenge your child or teen to resolve the problem. If necessary, persist, whispering encouragement to him or her to deal with the problem, offering help if needed by becoming an ally.

- Use a stage whisper technique often to check in with, analyze, and plan with the child; the whispering helps your adult support feel very separate and distinct from your character's voice.

- Use the sidebar technique often. Like an offline discussion in court, it can give you a chance to plan together or reflect on what is going on.

©istockphoto/McInnch

Examples

Stage whisper technique: You might whisper a narration or observation, "Yes, I see you're holding your food very tightly so the meat eater can't take it!" Then you could return to your role as the dinosaur and roar, "I'm hungry. *I want meat!*"

Sidebar technique: The child says, "Time for bed, doggy." Speaking as the pretend dog, you say, "I don't want to sleep! No sleep for me!" Then in a sidebar discussion with the child, you collaborate to plan together by clarifying, "Uh oh, he really doesn't want to sleep. He's going be so tired! What should we do?"

Dual roles: You can play the evil Borg drone as well as a Jedi knight in the same game as long as you use a different voice or body posture.

Enrich Play

5.7 Vary the forms of symbolic play

Why?

Forming and using symbols are capabilities that make human beings unique. The ability to engage in higher logic, math, creativity, invention, solutions to problems, as well as to reflect on emotions in oneself and others, all depend on this ability to form and use symbols. For this reason, broadening the *forms* of pretending and imagination enriches the child's or teen's mental life. Help children and adolescents use all different types of symbolic representation throughout the week.

How do we get there?

- Use your imagination to think of new play possibilities.

- For a child who limits symbolic play to toy figurines, encourage character role playing, cartoon drawing, spatial constructions (e.g., building a maze or a city), and so forth.

- For a teen who limits himself to verbal banter (hypotheses and theories), encourage joint film or play writing, creating alternate endings, scavenger hunts, simulation video games, what-if games, and so forth.

©istockphoto/ktaylorg

Examples

Construction: "How about we use blocks or draw so you can *show* me how their kingdom might be laid out?"

Drawing: "What if we draw our characters and then see if we can dress up like them?!"

Writing: "How would you end this book?"

Hypothesizing: "What if…there were no…maps? No mouths? No math? Now it's your turn to ask *me* a what-if."

Emotional and Logical Thinking

Making Sense of Oneself, Others, and the World

6A: Emotional Thinking

DIRFloortime® is a way for you to help your child or teen start down the road of emotional awareness, self-understanding, and reflection on emotional realities. Much of the time, this happens in the midst of imaginative play and reflective conversations, during which children and teens learn to experiment with and think about a widening array of emotional themes. The ultimate goals are emotional self-awareness, self-control, and empathy for others.

6B: Logical Thinking

You can be instrumental in the growth of logic by providing opportunities that help your child or teen make sense of the world and develop more insight, judgment, logic, and even wisdom. DIRFloortime is an approach to helping kids think through logical connections, wonder together, and attempt to explain why things are the way they are. Stanley Greenspan and Serena Wieder (2002) called this "building bridges between ideas"—between ideas of one's own as well as between one's own and the ideas of others. This ability lays the foundation for complex higher levels of thinking covered in the higher-level developmental capacities or DIR® Capacities 7–9. Attuned adults can support the emergence and robust expression of emotional and logical thinking by *challenging* children and adolescents to think via the following play-based and relationship-based strategies.

Strategies Include:

CHALLENGING—

6A: Emotional thinking

6.1. **Narrate:** Empathically narrate feeling states.
6.2. **Highlight emotions:** Emphasize the emotional aspects of life.

6.3. **Reflect:** Reflect on all feelings.

6.4. **Encourage empathy:** Help put on another's shoes.

6.5. **Play therapeutically:** Use play to help master overwhelming feelings.

6B: Logical thinking

6.6. **Build bridges:** Help build bridges between ideas.

6.7. **Elaborate:** Ask elaboration questions to encourage logical connections.

6.8. **Incite thinking:** Help your child or teen become an independent thinker

6.9. **Make connections:** Help the child or teen connect three or more ideas in a logical sequence.

6.10. **Event planner:** Sequence, plan, and communicate about the past and future.

6.11. **Organize and summarize:** Bring the child or teen back to the main idea.

6.12. **Debate:** Use debate to challenge the child or teen to connect ideas and develop logic.

Narrate

6.1 Empathically narrate feeling states

Why?

Narrating a child's thoughts and actions is an earlier strategy used to enhance regulation, engagement, purposefulness, and so forth, but here at Capacity 6 it is used to develop emotional self-awareness. Feeling known and being held in the mind of a loving caregiver is how our identity is formed and consolidated; having our feelings being felt and named by the other is what first helps us know what we are feeling and starts the process of figuring out how to take care of our difficult feelings. An understanding, observant adult can help children or teens connect their feelings to their causes and gain real emotional comprehension of self and eventually of others.

How do we get there?

- Empathize with or share what your child or adolescent seems to be feeling.

- *Resonate with it* rather than try to fix it or change it.

- Feel it and show it in your facial expressions and bodily expression.

- Don't be afraid to get it wrong—simply trying to name it promotes self-awareness.

- Often if you are not right, just trying to name it helps the child or adolescent clarify what the feeling is.

- State it rather than ask a question so that you instigate conversation and you don't put the child on the spot with what might feel a bit like a feelings quiz.

- Connect the feeling to its cause if you have a guess.

©istockphoto/Olgasea

Examples

Use simplified language: "Mad! Tower fell."

Use basic language: "You seem excited to go see Grandma!"

Use complex language: "I think you're mad at me for holding your brother when you wanted me to keep playing with the costumes with you."

Highlight Emotions

6.2 | Emphasize the emotional aspects of life

Why?

For children and adolescents who have developmental differences that make it harder for them to notice, comprehend, or manage emotions, we can emphasize the emotional realities in everyday life and in play. In stories, movies, and books, you can help call attention to the richness of the social world of emotions, and you can also begin to make the connections between feelings and the causes for feelings. This is using the curriculum of life to help advance skills in what may be a particularly challenging area.

How do we get there?

- Call attention to the emotional aspects of play scenarios, movies, conversation, games, and play themes.

- Point out, name, or explain emotional realities.

- Play the How Am I Feeling? game. Make faces and nonverbal gestures to express a feeling and then take turns guessing how the other players are feeling.

©GeDy Images/Digital Vision

CHALLENGING

Examples

With younger children: While at the park or other community interactive environment, narrate how the people around you seem to be feeling. For example, you might say, "Oh, that boy looks so sad. I think he scraped his knee."

With older children: During a movie or a book you could ask, "Hey, the brother got a new bike but his twin sister didn't. I wonder if she's feeling jealous?"

With adolescents: When discussing their friends, you can explain and remind about emotional realities, for example saying, "You said you were upset that he is going to stay with his grandparents all summer. How do you imagine he might be feeling about leaving? Maybe he has mixed feelings about this? Do you remember the mixed ways you felt when we thought we might be moving away but closer to your cousins? And how you felt when we stayed here?"

Reflect

6.3 Reflect on all feelings

Why?

Acceptance and a nonjudgmental attitude are required for the child or teen to learn to become curious about and aware of his or her feelings, both positive and negative. Parents' emotional *openness* has been shown to influence children's full integration of feelings and thoughts.

How do we get there?

- Emotional analysis: Invite the child or teen to reflect on feelings in play and in life, from both the child's or adolescent's side and the other's side.

- Social analysis: If the child or teen has difficult moments with peers, help explore his or her emotional responses.

- Self-reflection: Invite opinions more than facts.

Examples

Emotional analysis: "Remember when you were upset about the cat earlier today? Do you think you were mad? Or sad? Or something else?"

Social analysis: "What was it like for you when Gina walked away?" "Why do you think Tim is mean to kids?"

Self-reflection: "Who is your favorite character? Why?"

Encourage Empathy

6.4 Help put on another's shoes

Why?

One of the most difficult accomplishments in human experience, and one of the most important, is developing true empathy. Failures of empathy abound in adult life and society and cause extensive harm and suffering to others. To develop young people's critical social and moral capacity for taking another's perspective, attuned adults must provide extensive support to them. We can join with them and think aloud about the thoughts and emotions of others in their environment and in the world. Perspective taking and empathy are required in order to accurately interpret meanings and make good decisions in social interaction and even academic tasks.

How do we get there?

- Wonder together about people's thoughts, feelings, and motives.

- Ask questions about characters' thoughts, feelings, and motives while reading stories.

©Photodisc

Examples

With a preschooler: Invite young children to pretend to be someone else, then help them think about how that other person actually feels. Say, "You be the bus driver now. I'll be the kid getting on. How do you feel when some of the kids say 'good morning' to you?"

With a preteen: Play the Why Should I? game. When she wants you to do things for her, gently tease her with a response of "Why should I?" See how many reasons she can give you. Then offer a compromise such as, "Let's do it together."

With a teen: Help him remember a time when he strongly felt a similar emotion and connect this experience to what another person is feeling. Ask, "Remember what it felt like when Rebecca said no to your invitation? Do you think that maybe Max is feeling the same way when you say you are too busy to go shopping with him?"

Play Therapeutically

6.5 Use play to help master overwhelming feelings

Why?

Playing is the main way young people can explore and gain mastery over feelings that may otherwise seem too overwhelming to deal with. Play can help them get unstuck from either compulsively rehearsing or avoiding the memory. It's important for children to be able to play out their difficult feelings or for teens to deal with them by, for example, dramatizing, journaling, talking, or writing creatively about them. It can help to free and open up their minds to full emotional awareness. Child developmentalists have found that play that is watched and understood by a supportive, reflective adult develops children's ability to understand that their internal experience is only *one way* of viewing the external world and that there are other ways to view the same reality.

How do we get there?

- Watch play with interest.

- Even though it may be challenging for you at first, discipline yourself to encourage rather than shy away from or discourage difficult topics and themes that come up in play.

- Invite or entice the child or teen to explore topics you know are not being addressed through play.

- Gently help to show the possible connections between the play and real-life concerns so that self-reflection can grow.

©istockphoto/monkeybusinessimages

CHALLENGING

Examples

Fear: If a child accidentally saw a shooting on television and became frightened and fairly obsessed about it, support the topic in play rather than avoiding it, even though the play may feel repetitive and unpleasant to you.

Shame: Dolls or stuffed animals can go through pretend toileting accidents and embarrassment or frustration afterward, and you can support recognition of such feelings in these "others."

Loneliness: Ask the child or teen what would happen if his or her favorite character in a television show felt like he didn't have any friends at school, or what could be done if the character had a good friend move away.

Excitement: Puppets or stuffed animals may be used to dramatize all sorts of intense emotion at a sufficient emotional distance from the child that the intense emotions can be thought about more clearly.

Build Bridges

6.6 Help build bridges between ideas

Why?

Building bridges means beginning to use logic to put the world of ideas into a cause-and-effect framework for understanding the broader world. It also allows for interpersonal connections with other thinkers.

How do we get there?

- Look for opportunities in play and conversation.

- Use a "why and because" format to questions.

- Give multiple-choice options.

- Start by giving some silly options.

- Later provide several reasonable options.

©istockphoto/christingasner

CHALLENGING

Examples

Bridges can be built among various ideas about people, activities, and objects:

Invite the child or teen to build bridges from his or her ideas: "You want to get an ice cream cone? How come ice cream?"

Invite the child to build bridges with your ideas; make your toy truck swerve into a ditch and say, "Hey, what happened?" If no idea is offered, then suggest, "Do you think he blew a tire or saw a ghost and got scared?"

Invite hypothesizing: "I wonder what would happen if…"

Invite hypothesizing about feelings and thoughts in real life, books, movies, and play scenes: "Why do you think she did that?" "Would you feel the same way?"

Invite the child to build bridges between feelings: "You were playing with your friend, laughing and having fun, then all of the sudden you were sad. Did something go wrong in the game?"

Invite a teen to explain and connect: You could ask, "How was your day?" He or she might respond by saying, "Good." Then ask, "What made it a good day?"

Elaborate

6.7 Ask elaboration questions to encourage logical connections

Why?

We use elaboration questions to inspire children's and adolescent's emotional thinking and to support them in connecting the pieces of logical argument together. While compliance and cooperation are very important life skills, we must first help the child to think and reason before true compliance and cooperation are possible.

How do we get there?

- Instigate reflective discussions. When your child or teen wants something, don't simply say yes or no. Instead, ask what, when, why, and how types of elaboration questions. In this way, you'll help him or her give an opinion and reflect on his or her wishes.

- Explain why you want the child or teen to do something. Discuss the pros and cons, and give him or her plenty of time to argue a viewpoint. A good rule of thumb is that if your child's or teen's answers don't frequently surprise you, or if you have a single correct answer in mind, you are probably overscripting.

©istockphoto/bo1982

Examples

Elaborate together: While the child or teen is playing, ask him or her to elaborate on intentions. For example, ask, "Why are you driving the truck very slowly?"

Expose gaps: Challenge him or her to connect ideas. You could ask, "We were talking about the dance, but now you are telling me about the students arguing at lunch. What made you think of that?"

Find logic: Scaffold or give support as needed to draw out the intended purpose. Ask, "Wait a second. What did you mean just now?"

Incite Thinking

6.8 Help your child or teen become an independent thinker

Why?

Adults get into habits of imparting information: telling kids how to do things. These habits cause us to miss countless opportunities for helping children and teens develop independent capacities for logical thinking. Intellectual maturation and growth require daily opportunities for solving problems, experimenting, hypothesizing, designing, devising, and experiencing failure as well as success of planned projects. Following directions, repetitive practice, and rote memorization do not develop the intellectual adaptability needed for success in an ever more complex world.

How do we get there?

Always invite children and adolescents to think for themselves whether they are at school or at home in some of the following ways:

- Hypotheticals: Invite guessing and hypothesizing about possibilities. This stimulates better flow of ideas. Invite reflection, observation, and wonder.

- The big "Why": Why questions are the hardest but the most central for developing a logical sense of the world.

- Multiple choice: When asking questions, if open-ended questions are too difficult, give several alternative answers to choose from. In a difficult topic area, make the answer choice easier by giving some silly alternatives that are easy to reject.

Incite Thinking

©Shutterstock/Kris Jacbos

Examples

Hypotheticals: "I wonder why The Incredibles have different powers from each other if they are in the same family." "What do you think your friends would want to play if they were here right now?"

The big "Why": "Why do you think Dora was sad? Because Boots didn't listen to her? Or because he was eating his snack?"

Multiple choice: "Okay, it's a party for Pooh Bear. How do you think we could make it fun for him?" The child looks unable to answer. Add, "Do you think we should invite his friend Piglet? Or invite a scary Heffalump?"

Make Connections

<table>
<tr><td>6.9</td><td>Help the child or teen connect three or more ideas in a logical sequence</td></tr>
</table>

Why?

Logical connecting of ideas is the basis of making sense of ideas, people, the world, and oneself. It helps us separate reality from fantasy. It helps us make realistic plans to accomplish our goals. Supporting young people to make logical connections also works to help them begin to track and monitor the sequence and logic of their own thoughts, a very important later capacity.

How do we get there?

- Support: Help build a logical play sequence of ideas that follow from one another (not necessarily realistic).

- Clarify: Try making sense and meaning of the ideas and scenarios that the child or teen introduces by summarizing; asking clarifying questions; identifying the beginning, middle, and end of the story; and so forth.

- Order: Work on sequencing activities by talking about what comes first, next, and last in a play scene, book, or television show. Make a play plan to order fun activities as first, next, and last.

- Build bridges: When the child or adolescent switches plans without notice, try to highlight this and bring awareness as well as build a bridge between the prior thought and the new plan. The point is to help him or her monitor and evaluate his or her own connections and disconnections.

©istockphoto/robh

Examples

Support: "Okay, you said he is a little guy, and he can't find his mom, so he is probably feeling pretty scared. Do you think he could call out for someone to help him look for her?"

Order: "You said you are going to build a bridge and a tower, but do you think we need to dig the trench first for the bridge to go over?"

Clarify: Narrate whatever connections you can infer. "First we were playing this game, then suddenly you wanted to watch television. Hmmm, did playing this game remind you of a show you like?"

Build bridges: "Wait. You were being the tiger and now you want to watch the Thomas video. What happened? Maybe the tiger wants to race the train along the track?"

Event Planner

6.10 Sequence, plan, and communicate about the past and future

Why?

Working on sequencing and planning helps children and adolescents to develop organized, sequential thinking. It encourages planning ahead and executing ideas meaningfully in a logical flow.

How do we get there?

- Recount shared memories.

- Make future plans together.

- Follow a mutually developed list of activities.

- Talk about the sequence of the event's parts: "First we'll do this, and then what?"

- Involve the young person in making the plan for what to bring, wear, or do before you can start.

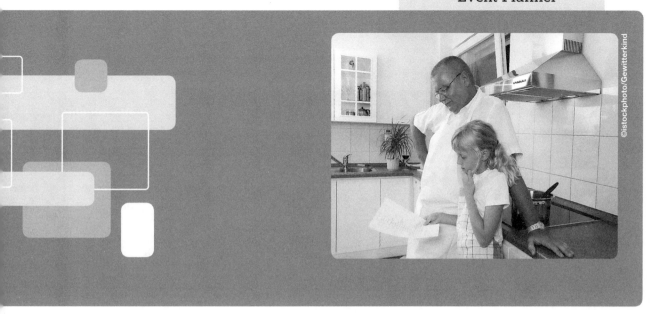

Examples

Preschoolers: Parents or teachers may take lots of pictures and then use those from past activities to help kids organize their thoughts about things they have done, places they have been, and things that have happened. Sit together and look through pictures, or put them in a photo book or digital album together while you talk about what you each remember, liked, and want to do again.

Elementary: Let them help to plan small events and big ones: "What should we play? And after we finish that, what next?" For a not-yet-verbal child: "You can help me pack the picnic—you can point to all the food and supplies you think we might need and then let's see how we can fit them into this cooler."

Teens: Invite reflection on the past and future planning using their favorite photo album online or in hand: "Do you remember what you liked about that adventure? What should we do on our next outing? What should we bring? What might be different about you or about the people or the place when we visit next time?"

Organize and Summarize

6.11 Bring the child or teen back to the main idea

Why?

When lots of information needs to be processed simultaneously, children and adolescents with developmental challenges are not always able to break the whole picture into meaningful units. Therefore, they often struggle to interpret objects, people, and surroundings as constituents of a whole situation, and they may tend to give too much focus to one or more details. As a result, they need a lot of support to be successful in processing all relevant parts of an idea at once and focusing on the main idea.

How do we get there?

- Support the original intent and help to hold the whole picture.

- Utilize methods of hinting or reminding of the main idea, such as sentence stems and linking words, without spelling it out completely.

- Wonder together: Use exaggerated mannerisms and hints to help connect back to the main idea.

- Utilize multiple forms of sensory input to help connect parts to the whole.

©Stockbyte

Examples

Wonder: Give a wondering expression and say, "Hmmm, I hear that you are thinking about cats right now, but we are really trying to describe what a *pet* is in *general*."

Warn: Use a finger in the air or a gentle "stop" hand gesture to indicate when a child or teen has gone too far into details and lost the listener or lost the point he or she was making.

Organize on paper: As the child or adolescent talks out some important topic, show how its parts relate. Write down key words in a conceptual bubble map, with the main idea in the middle.

Organize in space: Use bodily experience to support the understanding of a main idea. Walk together outside your house, apartment, or school and use the front door as the place to post or imagine the main idea as a name over the door. Post or imagine supporting ideas in interior rooms; place related or tangential ideas in closets.

Debate

Use debate to challenge the child or teen to connect ideas and develop logic

Why?

The overall approach to foster Capacity 6 rests on challenging children or adolescents and allowing them to experience more of the real you. Debate is a wonderful way to challenge and expand fledgling logical thinking skills as well as to present another person's perspective, opinions, and feelings, which can be understood to be separate and distinct.

How do we get there?

- Have lighthearted debates about everything from food and clothing choices to sharing toys.

- Remember, we are not working toward compliance as a priority until solid logical thinking is present. First, we must focus on developing logical understanding based on the ability to connect ideas. This requires that the young person is able to assert, challenge, and negotiate.

CHALLENGING

Examples

Debate club: Use a child's reluctance to make a transition as a reason to ask questions curiously. "*Why* do you want to stay up?" "*What* will it feel like when you get so tired?" "*How* do you think I feel about staying up?" Parents still get to make schedules and bedtimes, so start preparing for bedtime a bit earlier if possible in order to leave a window for this "debate" process.

Negotiate within limits: Sarah stops interacting when she gets a warning that play time is almost over. Her mother asks, "What's wrong?" Sarah replies, "Not done!" Sarah's mom says, "Ah, I see. You haven't finished building the castle. We have to get to the doctor on time or we won't get your medicine, so what should we do about the castle plans?" In this way, ongoing conversation flow is welcomed even while keeping up with a required schedule.

Strong opinions: Look for moments to let preteens and teens assert strong opinions and then have a friendly debate about your differing thoughts. For example, you might say something like, "You like their old songs way better than their newest one? What was better about the old ones? The new one makes me want to dance! It was the number one song on iTunes."

Complex Thinking

Multicausal, Gray-Area, and Reflective Thinking

Floortime works with children and teens to help them first develop solid foundational Capacities 1–6 and then move on to develop Capacities 7, 8, and 9, or complex thinking (Feder, 2009; Greenspan & Salmon, 1993; Greenspan, 2008; Robinson, 2011). These last three capacities describe the development of executive functioning, abstract thinking, and refined thought required for social and academic success in complex environments as well as the development of emotional and intellectual maturity needed to meet life's moral and emotional challenges. It describes the movement from being embedded in one's emotional experience to the freedom of being able to mentalize about ours and others' experience. In these stages, life with the child or teen gets even more interesting than before. Parents, educators, and therapists may help them move away from concrete, simplistic thinking and work toward differentiated or precise thinking and nuanced assessments of themselves and others.

Promote Multicausal Thinking

Why?

Capacity 7 describes the young person's evolution of psychological *mindedness*, or his or her continuing development of a *theory of mind. Multicausal and triangular thinking*, or DIR® Capacity 7, describes children's ability to see that there is more than one possible reason for things and more than one perspective as they begin to understand that peoples' internal experience is not the same as external reality. Once the first six milestones are solid, typically developing school-age children start to be able to accomplish this sort of thought. At this stage they even begin to understand that your and my differing perspectives are influenced by our prior experiences. This is necessary for perspective taking and empathy. A young person who is evidencing this multicausal and triangular thinking might be able to say, "My mom just came home talking on her phone and looks angry. Maybe she is mad because I left the door standing open again or maybe she is upset at the person on the phone. If it's a work call, she always has to sound nice and business-like to keep her job, but maybe on the inside she really doesn't like the person on the phone."

Develop Gray-Area Thinking

Why?

With Capacity 8 we are able to move from the world of concrete notions to abstract thinking. Rather than all-or-nothing categories for assessing self or others, at this eighth stage, called *gray-area thinking* or *relativistic thinking*, we see ourselves and others as driven by emotions and motives. We now see that those emotions have infinite variety and gradations of intensity that can be sorted in hierarchies and compared in terms of their relative importance in explaining behavior. Motivations or intentions can be multiple and conflictual; ambivalence can be identified. Arriving here means we understand that motives can be intentionally or unintentionally denied or hidden. Exceptions to the rule and sometimes versus always become distinguishable. Children on a typical developmental schedule may be evidencing the beginnings of Capacity 8 by the time they are in junior high school. An example of gray-area thinking might be: "I don't feel very good about myself at school because even though I'm proud of myself for pulling up my grades and grades are somewhat important to me, friends matter more, so it bothers me even more that I don't have friends there."

Encourage Reflective Thinking

Why?

Capacity 9 is the stable and flexible sense of self that allows for self-examination across a variety of situations and mental states, comparing oneself under different circumstances at different times, and comparing past, present, and future. *Reflective thinking* allows us to judge our experience and even to think from two different perspectives or two different frames of reference at once, which is required for empathic conflict resolution within oneself and in others. This stable sense of self allows one to have an internal standard of values and morality that acknowledges that while a certain choice may be acceptable for others it is not acceptable for oneself. It describes what is elsewhere described as mindfulness. Early high schoolers have the capability to achieve this level of thinking if they are helped to be solid in Capacities 1–8. Evidence of this level of reflective thinking might look like this: "When I'm around my parents, I feel pretty good about school because I know that they think that school is mainly about studying and grades, but when I get alone I start to feel bad about myself again because I'm not feeling very popular at school yet and for me the friendships are more important. Probably if I get to know some people better I'll start to get more confidence about the social thing."

Psychologists who study the process of development have discovered the importance of adults achieving these capacities for reflective thinking or *mentalizing* about children's intentions and feelings, as this helps their children to become secure, confident, and able to manage their strong emotions and impulses. The Floortime approach stresses the importance of DIR professionals seeking professional supervision of their work in order to grow ever more reflective themselves. This professional growth is essential if the professional is to support caregivers and parents to become more self-aware and aware of their children's internal experience; this awareness is what is required for parents to be able to help their children climb the social-emotional and intellectual ladder of development.

How do we get there?

- **Opinions:** Ask for the child's or teen's opinions and ask questions to which you don't know the answer.

- **Go for more:** When children or teens offer one cause, ask what other reasons might cause them or someone else to feel a certain way or might cause a situation.

- **More than one way to … :** When a solution is offered, say, "What could be another way to solve this?"

- **"Let's flex":** Use play and humor to invite flexibility in considering the perspectives of others.

- **Multiview:** Compare the different perspectives and viewpoints of various people whenever possible.

- **Gray matters:** Ask her to compare feelings with different feelings she may have, with others' feelings, and with her own similar feelings at other times.

- **Decisions:** Invite him to weigh the relative importance of feelings or determine which feeling matters most in a particular decision, such as what was the most important reason he chose to root for a particular team.

- **Internal versus external:** Ask questions about the interior life of your child and others and help her compare internal feelings to external behavior.

- **Real motives:** Wonder together about the multiple and various reasons for behavior, others' and one's own.

- **Let's qualify that:** Introduce emotions rating scales or feelings thermometers for the child or teen to identify how he is feeling right now in comparison with other moments.

- **Internal standard:** Provide categories for ways of assessing oneself and one's changing tendencies, such as alert versus sleepy, regulated versus dysregulated, introverted versus extroverted, conscientious versus expedient, visionary versus practical, and so forth.

- **Competing external standards:** Help young people consider and contrast the standards by which they evaluate and know themselves and others, particularly those standards and value systems that come from the self versus the family, versus the local community, and versus the larger society.

- **Follow up:** Check in on feelings at a later time and invite reflection on the causes of the emotions.

- **True reflection:** Share your observations about changes or differences in yourself and others.

- **Self-awareness:** Ask questions that invite your child or teen to be curious about herself.

Examples

- **Multicausal:** Your son is talking about a current court case discussed at school. Since he is showing an interest in this topic, you have a sense you can expand his thinking on this, so you ask, "What did you think of the verdict? Why do you think the jury decided that way? What might be another reason? What would you have done if you were on the jury? How would you vote if the accused was related to you? How much difference would that make?"

- **Multicausal:** Your student gets stuck insisting that there is only one right way to be fair—to be the same to everyone who is competing in an athletic contest at the school. You suggest there might be unusual circumstances that require different rules. You find it helps kids to think more flexibly if you ask them to imagine something wild, like "What if you were a Martian and had three light-sensitive eyes and no legs? Could the race rules be adapted for you? Would you want them to let you wear special sunglasses, too?"

- **Gray area:** A student is struggling to write a book report but doesn't know what to type. You get him to connect with the material emotionally and even physically and use that back-and-forth conversation to get him to think on a higher order. These are some of the starting questions you could use during the conversation, depending on what his ideas are: "What do you like about the book? Do you like it a lot or a little (show me with your hands)? Were there parts that bothered you in the story, and can you act out the part for me? Why do you think it bothered you? What could be another reason it bothered you? Did it bother you more than the other books you have read about kids with problems at school? Do you think it bothered you more than other kids who read this book? Why do you think so (or think not)? Do you think it bothered you more reading it this year than if you had read it 2 years ago? What has changed about you?"

- **Reflective:** Your daughter comes home from a sleepover. You ask, "Was it a good one this time?" She says it was but that it was a little sad at the end because her friend is going to a different school next year. "Were you more happy to be together or more sad she is not going to your school anymore?" She says, "Well, both, but I guess more happy." You ask, "Do you think you will feel more sad or less sad about her leaving once school starts up?" She thinks for a while and says that she doesn't know because her friend will obviously be missing, but she will be around all of her other friends. A question that she cannot answer yet still helps achieve the goal because it may percolate in her mind for a while and in the meantime lead to more pondering and self-reflection.

- **Reflective:** Review difficult moments using a curious tone and inquisitive language so you don't sound critical. For example, ask, "So, what do you think was happening for you? Is this typical for you or a little different? What might have been influencing you this time?" If your child or teen replies, "I don't know," you can invite a response by saying, "Take a guess."

- **Reflective:** Classmates are talking about a book they just finished. Ask them to think about the interior lives of the main characters and compare them to external reality. Ask, "How do you think the hero felt when he saw his first lion? What in his past might have made him feel that way? What other reasons might he have felt like that? What did it appear to his followers like he was feeling?"

- **Reflective:** Your preteen is starting to understand who he is as a person. You help that along in conversations about his changing feelings and yours. You might also check in days later to follow up on the feelings he shared and to extend the mutual reflection time. The conversation might go something like this:

You: "Are you not feeling like playing with the neighbors as much these days?"

Preteen: "Well, sometimes I don't feel like it."

You: "I've noticed that lately. You know, there are some neighborhood parents whom I feel closer to in certain situations or at certain times, like during the summer when we see more of each other and make the block party happen. When is it that you don't want to play with the kids around here?"

Preteen: "I don't know. Like, when I'm really bored it's okay, but otherwise I don't really want to."

You: "Are they not your type? They tend to be mostly pretty quiet when they come over. Do you think you like being with extroverts more?"

Preteen: "Well, I guess, yeah. I know I am . . . sort of . . . really . . . *not* an extrovert, but I seem to like loud, entertaining people a lot more, or else it gets just sort of boring getting together."

You: "You used to really love these friends. Did something change?"

Preteen: "I think I realized at school that I can be funny if the other kids are funny, but I don't have anything to say to people if they don't have anything to say, so then I feel awkward, so maybe that is why I don't feel like trying to go find them lately."

- **Reflective:** A couple presenting on a parent panel at a DIRFloortime® Coalition of California conference described their journey of finding a way to interact with their son based on his inner world rather than his outward, difficult behaviors. As he developed language, they were able to ask more about why he showed such resistance to certain transitions in his day. They described their own transformation, even in how they related to their other child, by adopting Floortime's focus on developing a child's intentionality. The parents showed old video of the mom working with her son around his resistance to getting dressed through playful support, gentle encouragement, and her own sense of there being a legitimate emotional reason for his difficult behavior. Afterward, they interviewed their then 11-year-old son about his thoughts about his growth through Floortime. He was able to compare his different feelings for the various Floortime interventionists who had worked with him at home and at school. His mother also asked him specifically why he used to get so dysregulated when it was time to get dressed to go out. He was able to describe the confusion and resulting upset he'd had in the past about the meaning of time and then compare the past feelings to how he feels now about cooperating with a time schedule.

Reducing Problem Behaviors

Clinical and research evidence shows that problem behaviors are significantly reduced over time when caregivers or teachers consistently use Floortime strategies (DeWaay, Davis, & Clements, 2010, Greenspan & Wieder, 1997). When a child or teen receives developmental, relationship-based intervention, or DIRFloortime®, problem behaviors are gradually replaced by positive coping strategies and more productive activity. Nevertheless, families worry about how to reduce problem behaviors in the meantime. Habits such as darting away, non-compliance with parents, tantrums, aggression, and repetitive behaviors cause particular concern because these behaviors often disrupt the possibility of positive family experiences or outside social opportunities. What follow are strategies for addressing problem behaviors directly. These strategies were taken from *How to Talk So Kids Will Listen and Listen So Kids Will Talk*, by A. Faber and E. Mazlish; *Treating Explosive Kids*, by R.W. Greene and S.J. Ablon (2006); *The Child with Special Needs*, by S. Greenspan and S. Wieder (1998); *Descriptive Praise: The #1 Motivator for Children*, by N. Janis-Norton (2006); and *Calmer, Easier, Happier Parenting*, also by N. Janis-Norton (2012).

Strategies Include:

REDUCING PROBLEM BEHAVIORS—

X.1. **More Floortime:** Increase Floortime play proportional to increased expectations and challenges.

X.2. **Find behavioral clues:** View behavior as a meaningful clue.

X.3. **Choose behaviors:** Choose and target the most important behaviors.

X.4. **Take manageable steps:** Teach new behaviors in manageable steps.

X.5. **Make modifications:** Modify the schedule and the environment to reduce the likelihood of problem behaviors.

X.6. **Notice and mention:** Notice and mention all the small steps in the right direction.

X.7. **Preview:** Rehearse and preview expected behaviors and new situations.

X.8. **Post rules:** Agree on, post, and enforce written household rules.

X.9. **Provide visuals:** Provide visual reminders and visual schedules.

X.10. **Provide support:** Provide empathic responses to expressions of negative emotion.

X.11. **Grant wishes:** Grant a wish imaginatively.

More Floortime

X.1 Increase Floortime play proportional to increased expectations and challenges

Why?

DIR® is a developmental ladder approach—it asks you to strengthen foundations before building higher skills. Thus, before you tackle problems such as an eating-refusal problem or a nighttime waking problem, transition to a new school, or an anxiety-producing dental procedure, shore up the foundations of the empowering relationship with more Floortime play sessions. This also allows children and adolescents to express their feelings about the increased demands, expectations, and especially doubts about their own competence or fears they may fail or disappoint their parents or teachers.

How do we get there?

- Schedule one-to-one and family play sessions on your calendar.

- Set aside all potential distractions to you and to the child (e.g., electronics, pets, extraneous people, phones).

- Label these sessions in order to highlight them and to help the child or teen look forward to these times. (You may call them "Special Time," or choose your own fun name.)

- Suggest play themes related to the new challenge or to related self-doubts to see if the child or teen is willing to explore the challenges in play.

- Empathize with the child's or teen's concern about failure or about disappointing you.

©istockphoto/akurtz

Examples

Increasing Floortime is easily geared to children of different ages:

Preschool: A 4-year-old is going to start attending a preschool program, so starting 4 weeks ahead, the parents add an extra Floortime play session each morning and evening in order to strengthen their relationship and to offer opportunities to explore feelings about separation, a new teacher, new children, a new setting, and any possible fears about success, failure, or overwhelming challenges.

Elementary: An 8-year-old's family is expecting a second child soon. Floortime sessions scheduled into the family routine before *and* after the baby arrives will really support the child in adapting to the changes. Play and conversation can address the myriad of mixed feelings that may arise when a newcomer adds to the joy but requires extensive attention and time of the adults.

High school: A ninth-grade student is going to be included in general education classes for math for the first time in a number of years. He is anxious about the noise and class size but eager to learn math skills. His aide asks the parent to pack the teen a sack lunch each day so they can eat quickly and then have time to walk the track and talk about how things are going before heading to math after lunch.

Find Behavioral Clues

X.2 | View behavior as a meaningful clue

Why?

Human beings make sense. If we view difficult behaviors as clues to what a child needs, we are halfway toward a solution that gets to the root of the problem. This perspective also greatly reduces parental and teacher frustration and stress. Interacting with children and adolescents in a way that communicates that their intentions make sense to us also helps them to grow in their ability to make sense of themselves and their own underlying intentions and mental states.

How do we get there?

- Get curious—wonder what might be behind a child's misbehavior.

- Remind yourself that there may be a good reason a child has initially gotten into a habit of misbehavior even if it no longer has good outcomes.

- Think about what triggers the behavior.

- Think about what might be achieved by the behavior.

©istockphoto/guter

Examples

Clues can be found in the environment, in relationships, or elsewhere:

If your son or daughter tends to make repetitive vocalizations, wonder about when this tends to occur most. If you notice that it seems to happen most often in loud social settings, think about what he or she is trying to accomplish in this setting. You might hypothesize that this behavior is a way to feel more in control of intense (startling) auditory input. If so, you could offer an alternative way of controlling the intense input (e.g., noise cancelling headphones, planned breaks from the environment) and then see if the loud vocalizations would then not be needed so much.

Choose Behaviors

X.3   Choose and target the most important behaviors

Why?

Learning new behavior is difficult. If a parent tackles too much work with the child or teen at once, he or she will become a stressor, and the attachment or mental habit of turning toward the parent for comfort will be compromised.

How do we get there?

- Decide if a problem behavior is urgent or can wait a while.

- Choose the most disruptive, problematic behavior to start with, and the positive results of improvement will give energy to the parent and child to tackle smaller issues later (see Janis-Norton, 2012).

- Figure out the purpose for the behavior and help meet that purpose in more adaptive ways.

- Teach one to two foundational behaviors that affect all the others: for example, cooperating with adults and not hurting others.

Examples

Darting versus rudeness: Parents of twins decide that darting away is the urgent behavior to address but that the children's being rude to one another is a behavior that can be tackled later. They figure out the reason for darting in one twin is to get the other to chase, so they label the game Chase and let the children play it in the fenced backyard before taking walks. On the walks, they let everyone who "stays together" take turns being the leader.

Hurting versus manners: The child is biting and hitting his one-to-one aide when he gets either happily excited or upset, and the child is also constantly picking his nose (which can be embarrassing for families). Address "keeping others safe" as the chosen behavior to work on and let go of the nose picking for now. Hold the boundary of "no hurting," but explore and find things together that *can* be safely hit or bitten.

Take Manageable Steps

 X.4 Teach new behaviors in manageable steps

Why?

Learning new skills can be simplified and made less stressful for children, teens, and families if new skills are approached in small, systematic steps.

How do we get there?

- Think about all skills as combinations of component "microskills" (see Janis-Norton, 2012).

- Give lots of encouragement and support for practicing the small steps.

- Practice the easiest piece of a new skill first (often the last step in a sequence).

©Veer/Fancy Photography

Examples

Almost all activities can be broken down into manageable steps:

Young child: Sleeping independently depends on putting oneself back to sleep after awakenings. Help the child learn to do this on his or her own by withdrawing your sleep support (e.g., touch, your immediate presence, backrubs) very gradually over days or weeks if needed.

School-age child: Teaching a child to tie a bow can best be done by practicing the final step of the bow first and then working back through the steps.

Older child: Teaching an older child to use a dictionary starts with first getting the child secure through daily practice in recalling alphabetical order.

Make Modifications

Modify the schedule and the environment to reduce the likelihood of problem behaviors

Why?

It is important to design and *simplify* the home environment and *lighten* scheduling in ways that increase the ease of the child or adolescent's success and reduce everyone's agitation. As the environment and schedule are modified, families will see greater success on the child's or teen's part as well as on the parents' part. The point of such modifications is to make it much easier for the young person to behave in mature ways.

How do we get there?

- Simplify the home, car, and school environment.

- Reflect on your child's, your teen's, and even your own reaction to your surroundings in order to gain insight into ways you can adapt the visual or auditory environment to ensure the young person's successes more often at home.

- Lighten the schedule by greatly reducing everyone's voluntary commitments to free up more time for sufficient sleep and for getting ready at a relaxed pace—parents and their offspring are all at their worst when sleep derived or having to race the clock.

Examples

Environment:

Create a safe place to go at school or home when feeling overwhelmed (e.g., pillow corner, tent).

Provide sensory objects and tools that children can utilize while they interact (e.g., exercise ball, chewy objects, squeeze ball, mini-trampoline).

Remove constant sources of family conflict or danger in the environment.

Organize and label toys and supplies to aid in cleaning up or finding things.

Show and preview a visual schedule of daily routines to support the child or teen and prevent recurring (thus predictable) misbehaviors.

Schedule:

Prepare ahead and allow *plenty of time* to wake up, get ready, and travel to school or activities because daily nagging to rush people doesn't typically increase success.

Remove likely distractions, such as activities involving electronic screens, from the morning routine.

Plan sensory breaks such as playdough sessions, dancing, or bouncing in between homework "focus time" periods.

Provide favorite activities or toys a child or teen can look forward to after difficult tasks (e.g., homework, teeth brushing, calming down).

Lighten outside commitments to allow recommended amounts of sleep: 12 hours per day for preschoolers, 10 for children, 9 for teens, and 8 for adults.

Notice and Mention

X.6 Notice and mention all the small steps in the right direction

Why?

"Descriptive praise," or "noticing and mentioning" *all* the improvements your child or teen is making, is one of the most powerful methods teachers and parents can use (Janis-Norton, 2006). Descriptive praise helps children and adolescents create better habits because it motivates them to try harder to do better. It even works with adults, so you may definitely want to make this a habit in adult relationships as well. Descriptive praise makes it easier for everyone to do better because it helps build a self-concept based on actual, real-life successes.

How do we get there?

- **Be on the lookout:** Describe all the improvements you see and appreciate.

- **Don't stop:** Notice and mention *every* small improvement and keep up a running commentary.

- **Avoid the negative:** But *do* remember to point out the *absence* of negative behaviors.

- **Label it:** Use the instance of improvement to point out its evidence of a general character trait.

- **Keep it up:** Descriptive praise must be used consistently and liberally to work. Notice and mention positives all throughout every day.

- **Don't evaluate:** Research shows that the use of such global evaluations as "You're so smart!" demotivates young people.

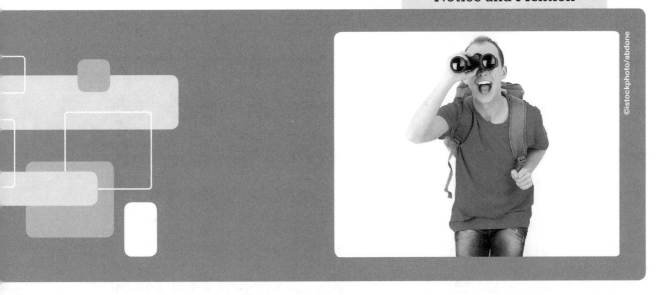

©istockphoto/abdone

- **Don't use overly positive evaluations:** Such exclamations as "That's fantastic!" almost always get discounted or dismissed by young people as well as adults—don't hurt your credibility.

- **Don't thank:** Thanking makes it seem like positive behaviors are favors for you. For this method, don't start by mentioning your feelings about the improvements because this distracts from the purpose of children and adolescents forming an image of themselves as capable.

Examples

Be on the lookout: When your child or teen responds well to your request, say, "You listened the first time I asked you to clean up the toys with me."

Don't stop: "I noticed that you washed your hands without my reminding you!"

Avoid the negative: "You remembered not to drop your shoes in the kitchen today." "You got really mad, but you made a good choice to talk yourself down instead of hitting."

Label it: "You talked it out with your brother and remembered he doesn't like it if you scream at him; that shows maturity." "You came back this way when I called your name. That's cooperation."

Preview

Rehearse and preview expected behaviors and new situations

Why?

The process of rehearsing or visualizing expected behavior and new, challenging situations is required for young people to truly understand an expectation. True understanding must come first, and then more consistent cooperation is possible. Too often parents just hope for the best and get upset or disappointed when behavior is poor. When children or teens verbalize the expectation, either orally or through pointing or typing, they picture themselves doing what is expected. This visualization makes the new habit or behavior much easier to accomplish. Noel Janis-Norton (2012) calls this a "think-through."

How do we get there?

- Walk through, talk through!

- Help *visualize and verbalize* household rules in neutral or happy contexts.

- Help practice new expected behaviors in advance.

- Have child or teen talk through rules or new expectations many times per day, especially when you are teaching a new habit or introducing a new rule.

- Practice for new or unfamiliar experiences at home or away well in advance.

©Corbis

Examples

Preverbal child: "Show me how you are going to hold on to me in the parking lot." "Show how you will hold on to the basket at the store." "Show me what we are going to do first when we get to their house, before we go inside."

Partially verbal child: "Let's say the rule together: No hurting ANYONE!"

Verbal child: "There is a new rule. Starting next Monday, you will finish your meal before you climb down to play. So now it's your turn: When is the new rule starting? You're right—Monday. Now it's your turn to tell me the rule. Great, you remembered the rule."

Teen: "Before you head out, tell me the curfew and what you will do just *before* curfew."

Post Rules

X.8 Agree on, post, and enforce written household rules

Why?

Cooperation and family harmony is greatly improved when caregivers in the home compromise together and agree on what the rules will be, write the rules down for everyone to remember, and then make sure the rules are followed each time they are applicable. Clear expectations increase the consistency of children's *and* parents' follow-through. Young people feel safe when their caregivers show the fortitude to set reasonable limits and withstand the force of their protests. They feel contained when they know the boundaries and limitations within their environment and relationships. All people are much more willing to cooperate when rules are clear in advance and enforced every time.

How do we get there?

- Start by determining the values you agree that you most want to instill and then articulate the do's and don'ts that develop the habits that reflect those values (Janis-Norton, 2012).

- Be sure to agree on and then write down consistently enforceable consequences.

- Give warning of household rule changes several days or even a week ahead.

- Post rules in the house so children and teens can reference them on their own (use words and symbols) and so parents can remember exactly what was decided.

Examples

Self-control: If someone gets hurt, wrestling is over for the day.

Safety: If you forget to walk together with a parent, you have to ride in the stroller.

Kindness: No hurting anyone or anything.

Respect: If you forget to ask politely, the answer will be "no."

Self-organization: When you finish a chore, report back in to tell us what you did before you start something else.

Accomplishment: Finish homework before playtime.

World awareness: Read a news story every day.

Provide Visuals

X.9 Provide visual reminders and visual schedules

Why?

Adding visual communication to oral communication supports comprehension. Providing visual supports decreases anxiety about and resistance to new situations, increases agency and autonomy by allowing independent access to important information, and helps promote organization in thinking and planning.

How do we get there?

- Keep a large desktop or wall calendar to place stickers on or on which to draw pictures of upcoming events.

- Post daily schedule and weekly schedule, using pictures if needed.

- Break down challenging activities (e.g., getting dressed, going potty, cleaning room) into ministeps and post photos of child completing each step.

- Use a variety of media to prepare your child for upcoming events (e.g., books on the topic, physical rehearsals).

- Create a personalized book (digital or physical format) using Social Stories (Gray, 2010; see http://www.thegraycenter.org) to help your child understand a new expectation or difficult social concept.

©istockphoto/omgimages

Examples

Take advantage of all opportunities to reference the posted rules and schedules:

Morning: "Great, you cleared your dishes! What's next? Check your picture schedule!"

Afternoon: "Six more days before you go see the dentist. Let's color them on the calendar."

Evening: "Time to lay out your clothes for tomorrow. Let's use your clothes to build a flat 'person' on the floor—we need the shirt and the pants, and should she wear a hat? What's missing?"

Provide Support

 Provide empathic responses to expressions of negative emotion

Why?

Providing empathic reflection of feelings, or showing with your face, body, and words that you feel and understand what the child or teen is feeling, can be the most powerful first response. For young people or adults, receiving empathy helps regulate emotional responses and promotes emotional self-awareness. Well-timed active listening, or letting the child or teen feel that he or she is "felt," can deescalate an emotional meltdown, and this sort of coregulation also leads over time to better identity consolidation, self-regulation, and emotional resilience.

How do we get there?

- **Active listening:** Show concern and understanding for your child's negative emotion through facial expressions as well as sounds or words that communicate understanding.

- **Sensitive timing:** When the child or teen is cooled down, summarize how you think he or she is feeling.

- **Resist the urge:** Don't give in to the temptation to reassure, defend your position, or explain in order to try to get rid of the feelings—that usually backfires and certainly doesn't contribute to emotional maturation.

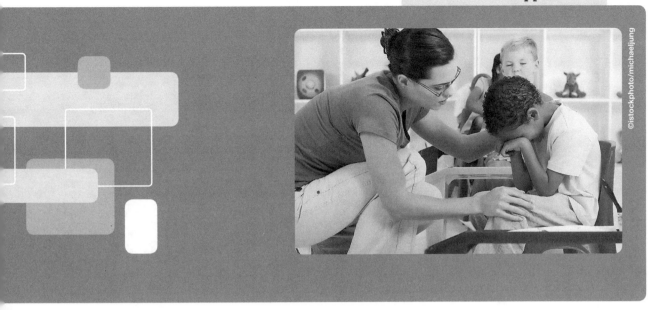

©istockphoto/michaeljung

Examples

Preschooler: In an empathic tone that matches the child's intensity but does not sound angry, say, "You feel really, really, really angry!"

School-age: If child is angry and lashing out physically, it is important both to set safety limits and to communicate your support and understanding, Say. "You are *so* mad! I see how much you want to hit something—you can't hit me, but you can *tell me* how mad you are."

Teen: Say, "It seems like you might be pretty worried about going—maybe you're worried about whether you will like any of the people there."

Grant Wishes

 **X.11** Grant a wish imaginatively

Why?

Granting a wish in fantasy, as described in the classic parenting guide, *How to Talk So Kids Will Listen and Listen So Kids Will Talk* (Faber & Mazlish, 2012), is a concrete demonstration of empathy; it shows that we both accept and understand how children are feeling if we suggest imaginative scenarios in which they can have their wishes granted in a grand way. Another benefit for children who may have developmental challenges is that it invites more practice with the imagination in a very highly motivating way since this helps the child imagine satisfying an intense emotional desire in the moment. Furthermore, it is a powerful co-regulating strategy since two hearts holding the same wish can manage disappointment of the wish easier than one alone.

How do we get there?

- If your child is frustrated, grant the wish in the imaginative realm in order to demonstrate your full empathic understanding. This is not a time to teach a lesson or moralize, just empathically wish together. When supported in this way, kids or teens are more able to see the logic or morals on their own once they feel better.

Grant Wishes

©Veer/Fancy Photography

Examples

Preschooler: "You want ice cream so bad right now, I bet you wish you could eat a whole ice cream store!"

Elementary: "You're sad because you can't play with your cousins. Don't you wish you had a private jet and could fly right now to their house, play with them a while, then fly back home for dinner?"

Middle school: "Maybe we could get the president to pass a new law making all schools illegal!"

High school: "I think you probably would prefer to have this whole house to yourself."

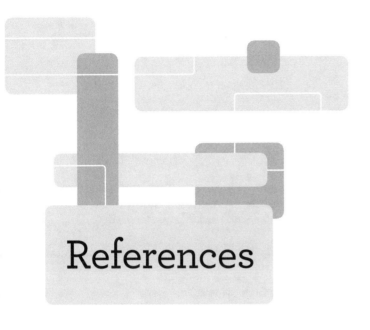

References

Bowlby, J. (1940). The influence of early environment on neurosis and neurotic character. *International Journal of Psychoanalysis, XXI*, 1–25.

Casenhiser, D., Shanker, S., & Stieben, J. (2013). Learning through interaction in children with autism: Preliminary data from a social-communication-based intervention. *Autism, 17*, 220–241.

DeWaay, R., Davis, A., & Clements, M. (2010). Parents' Perceptions of Treatment Effectiveness for Autism Symptoms in a DIR/Floortime Home Intervention. Presented to Autism 2010, Toronto, November, 2010.

Faber, A. & Mazlish, E. (2012). *How to talk so kids will listen and listen so kids will talk.* New York, NY: Scribner.

Feder, J. (2009). *ICDL SoCal Talk 7 Ate 9.* Retrieved from http://circlestretch.com/dir-training-materials/icdl-socal-talk-7-ate-9

Gray, C. (2010). *The new Social Story book: 10th anniversary edition.* Arlington, TX: Future Horizons.

Greene, R.W., & Ablon, S.J. (2006). *Treating explosive kids: The collaborative problem-solving approach.* New York, NY: Guilford Press.

Greenspan, S. (2008). *The "Greenspan" floortime model.* Retrieved from http://www.scribd.com/doc/3046558/floor-time

Greenspan, S., & Salmon, J. (1994). *Playground politics: Understanding the emotional life of your school-age child.* Boston, MA: Da Capo Press.

Greenspan, S., & Wieder, S. (1997). Developmental patterns and outcomes in infants and children with disorders in relating and communicating: A chart review of 200 cases of children with autistic spectrum diagnoses. *The Journal of Developmental and Learning Disorders, 1,* 1–38.

Greenspan, S., & Wieder, S. (2002). DIR®: Stages in Functional Emotional and Intellectual Development. Retrieved from http://astrafoundation.org/Min%20iFDL%20Poster_regular%20graphics.pdf

Greenspan, S., & Wieder, S. (2006). *Engaging autism: Using the Floortime approach to help children relate, communicate and think.* Boston, MA: Da Capo Press.

Greenspan, S., & Wieder, S. (1998). *The child with special needs.* Boston, MA: Da Capo Press.

Janis-Norton, N. (2012). *Calmer, easier, happier parenting: Simple skills to transform your child.* London, UK: Hodder & Stoughton.

Janis-Norton, N. (2006). *Descriptive praise: The #1 motivator for children* [CD]. London, UK: The New Learning Centre.

Kranowitz, C.S. (1998). *The out of sync child.* New York, NY: Skylight Press.

Main, M., Kaplan, K., & Cassidy, J. (1985). Security in infancy, childhood, and adulthood: A move to the level of representation. In I. Bretherton & E. Watters (Eds.), *Growing Points of Attachment Theory and Research, Monographs for the Society of Research in Child Development, 50*(1-2, Serial No. 209), 66–104.

Pajareya, K. & Nopmaneejumruslers, K. (2011). A pilot randomized controlled trial of DIR/Floortime intervention for pre-school children with autistic spectrum disorders. *Autism, 15,* 563–577.

Robinson, R. (2011). *Autism solutions: How to create a healthy and meaningful life for your child.* Don Mills, Ontario, Canada: Harlequin Books.

Solomon, R., Necheles, J., Ferch, C., & Bruckman, D. (2007). Pilot study of a parent training program for young children with autism: The P.L.A.Y. Project Home Consultation program. *Autism, 11,* 205–224.

Wallin, D.J. (2007). *Attachment in psychotherapy.* New York, NY: Guilford Press.

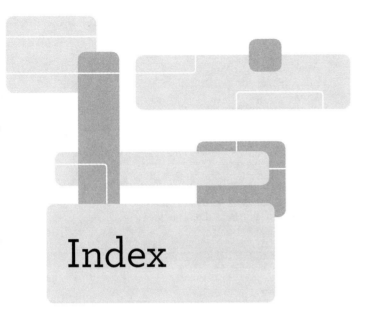

Index

Note: Figures indicated by *f*.